SERIAL KILLERS RAGE AND HORROR

8 Shocking True Crime Stories of
Serial Killers and Killing Sprees

Serial Killers Anthology

By

Jack Rosewood & Rebecca Lo

DISCLAIMER:

This serial killer anthology explores eight different cases of serial killers. It is not the intention of the author to defame or intentionally harm anyone involved. The interpretation of the events leading up to the discovery of the murders, are the opinion of the author as a result of researching these true crime killers. Any comments made about the motive and behavior of each killer is the sole opinion and responsibility of the author.

Free Bonus!

Contents

Introduction

The world is full of mass murders, spree killers, and serial killers. As the population continues to grow globally, the numbers are increasing. Some consider spree and mass killers to be the worst kind of murderers - those that in one moment enter a building where there are a lot of people and open fire, killing as many as quickly as possible. But those kinds of murders are often over in a matter of minutes. Serial killers can instill fear in the communities for years, in some cases decades, and for many people, these are the worst of them all.

Anatoly Onoprienko is perhaps one of the worst serial killers known so far. A cold, vicious killer, he terrorized the Ukraine as he slaughtered families in their beds at night. Then there are killers like Fritz Haarmann and Ronald Dominique who abducted, raped and killed numerous young boys and men for their own guilty pleasures. But these men aren't that different in reality - all were monsters who preyed on innocent people, ripping them from their families and friends at their own will.

Spree or mass killers have been in the news media in recent years as they seem to be occurring more often. In the last 50 years, there have been many incidents of men going on rampages in

1

schools, universities and restaurants, with high kill rates and often ending in suicides. Cho Seung-Hui, George Hennard and James Huberty all have this in common. There were warning signs for each of them, but nobody realized the damage they were about to inflict.

This book delves into eight cases involving serial, spree and mass killers, some of who are well-known and others that are perhaps not as famous. In each case we will look at the perpetrator and his background history, the crime, and examine the reasons behind the atrocities they committed. But we won't forget about the victims either. Often the focus is on the man behind the trigger instead of the person on the receiving end of the bullet. In many of these cases, the victims' names and details are included.

The killers in this book are the stuff of nightmares. Real-life bogeymen that had the ability to strike anytime, anywhere, and without notice. They all left a trail of carnage so horrific, and a number of victims so high, that they are right at the top of the list when it comes to murderers. The crimes they committed not only changed the way people lived, but also resulted in law changes to protect the innocent, in the hopes of preventing such tragedies from occurring again.

CHAPTER 1:

David Parker Ray – The Toy Box Killer

David Parker Ray – kidnapper, rapist, inflictor of gruesome torture, and killer. In Elephant Butte, near the ironically named town of Truth and Consequences, Ray created a place where he could carry out his sexually sadistic fantasies for more than forty years. This place would come to be known as the toy box, and the horrors women endured within are beyond comprehension. Although it is suspected Ray had committed up to sixty murders, no bodies have ever been found. However, victims who escaped the toy box would ultimately lead to his capture, and it would be discovered that he didn't act alone.

A Bullied Boy

Ray was born to parents Cecil and Nettie in Belen, New Mexico, on November 6, 1939. The family was poor, and at the time they were living on a ranch belonging to Nettie's parents. Later, a second child would be born, Peggy. The household was dysfunctional, with Cecil regularly getting drunk and physically abusing his children and his wife. By the time Ray was 10 years old, Cecil left the family and eventually divorced Nettie.

Struggling to manage the children, Nettie sent both children to live on their grandparents' ranch in Mountainair. Life changed dramatically for both Ray and his sister Peggy, as Ethan Ray, their grandfather, was very strict, and although he was almost 70 years old, he ruled the household. If the children didn't meet his standards or if they broke the rules, they would be physically disciplined. The children still saw their father from time to time, but he continued to inflict abuse upon them.

The bullying Ray suffered at the hands of his family members was soon continued by his peers as he entered his teenage years. Ray was tall, and a little awkward, and was very shy around girls. He didn't fit in with his schoolmates, and he was continuously bullied because of his shyness and inability to even talk to girls. As a result, Ray would spend most of his time on his own instead of socializing with other children. It wasn't long before he started to abuse drugs and alcohol, and his sexual fantasies took a disturbingly dark turn.

These fantasies were centered on bondage, rape, torture, murder, and other acts of sadomasochism. His sister Peggy would later mention that she had once come across some of Ray's drawings and photographs, all with the same erotic and disturbing themes. Despite her discovery, there are no reports to suggest anything was done about Ray's behaviors. In fact, he would later join the Army, where he worked as a general mechanic before being honorably discharged.

Ray would later tell his fiancée that his first murder occurred when he had only just become a teen. He claimed that after tying a woman to a tree, he then tortured her before killing her. This has never been quantified as being true, and it's possible that this was also another of his fantasies.

The Toy Box

Following his discharge from the Military, Ray set in motion his plan to create his dream torture room, where he could carry out all of his sadistic fantasies. The first step was to purchase an old motor home which he filled with a wide variety of torture tools, such as chains, whips, pulleys, clamps, straps, saws, surgical blades and leg spreaders. There was also an old gynecology chair, sex toys, syringes, and a mirror on the ceiling. He liked to call this his 'toy box', and an electrical generator was used to run the other devices he needed to inflict pain.

A number of detailed diagrams were attached to the walls of the toy box, all of which depicted different techniques and methods for inflicting pain on someone. The mirror was on the ceiling because Ray wanted his victims to be able to see exactly what he was doing to them. While in the toy box, his victims would be forced to listen to an audio recording of his voice during the periods they were conscious.

It is estimated Ray spent over $100,000 on his toy box, and it would be first put to use at some point during the 1950s. He kidnapped a woman and drugged her before taking her back to his torture chamber. There, she would endure being sexually assaulted and tortured for many days until he tired of her and murdered her. Ray would continue to kidnap, mutilate and murder multiple victims for the next forty years, until one miraculously escaped and his deeds were discovered.

Decades of Depravity and Murder

For four decades Ray had kidnapped women, often prostitutes, taken them back to his toy box and done whatever his sick mind wanted to them. It's incredible he was able to get away with it for so long, something he accredited to drugging the women with drug cocktails to ensure they suffered amnesia. Not all of his victims were killed; they simply either couldn't remember the details or were too humiliated to come forward. Until, that is, one incredibly brave woman made a break for freedom and succeeded.

Cynthia Vigil

In 1999, Cynthia was working as a prostitute in Albuquerque when she came into contact with Ray. He had asked her to perform oral sex on him in exchange for $20, and she agreed, going willingly with him to his vehicle. Once they were inside, a woman helped Ray tie her up and gag her, and around her neck they placed a metal collar. For the next hour or so, they traveled in the vehicle until coming to a stop at a motor home, where they proceeded to drag Cynthia inside and onto a bed, her hands chained to the bed post.

A taped recording was played where a male voice told her she was a now a sex slave and she should never speak unless asked to. She was instructed to call Ray 'master' and the woman who was helping him 'mistress'. The tape chillingly went on to explain she would remain naked and chained, in effect treated like a dog. She would be raped, tortured, be forced to have sex with animals, have her anus penetrated with large sex toys, and her body would be positioned in certain ways to expose her genital areas. The recording also informed her that there had been other slaves who were eventually set free if they cooperated, but if she didn't, she would be killed. She was also shown a videotape of another woman enduring horrific abuse at the hands of her captor.

Over the next three days, Cynthia had been whipped, shocked by electricity, cattle prodded, and had a variety of sex toys and medical instruments inserted into her rectum and vagina. Ray raped her repeatedly, including while she was strung up and chained to the ceiling. Convinced she was going to die soon, Cynthia looked for an opportunity to escape, and that soon presented itself, when Ray left the toy box at one stage and she was able to get hold of the keys.

Once she had unlocked the chain that was holding her captive, Cynthia desperately made a call to 9-1-1, but Ray's female accomplice tried to stop her. A fight between them ensued, and Cynthia eventually stabbed her in the neck with an ice pick that was nearby. Then she ran. Wearing only the metal collar around her neck and iron shackles around her ankles, Cynthia kept running until she saw a mobile home with its front door open. She ran inside, covered in blood, and begged the homeowner to call the police.

The police responded quickly, and could see from the state of Cynthia's body that the story she was telling them was true. Her body was covered in wounds inflicted by Ray – burns, bruises, cuts and puncture wounds were clearly evident. Cynthia was unsure where she was, but was able to give the officers information on where to find Ray and his torture chamber. However, because they had received a hang-up call from that location, police were already there and Ray was arrested.

Angelica Montano

Although Cynthia's body and condition bore the hallmarks of torture and abuse, the police were still unsure how true her story was. This was largely because she had admitted to being a prostitute and that she had initially gone with Ray willingly. However, once her story and Ray's arrest made headlines, another victim stepped forward to back up her story. That victim was Angelica Montano.

According to Angelica, she too had been kidnapped by Ray and his female accomplice, now known to be Cindy Hendy, Ray's girlfriend. For three days, Angelica had been raped repeatedly and tortured before being drugged and dumped on the side of the highway in the desert. Police found her at the time and took down her complaint, but for reasons unknown, the police never followed up on her accusations. The complaint just seemed to disappear, and Angelica only decided to try again when she saw Cynthia's story on the news.

Kelly Garrett

While investigating the claims of Cynthia and Angelica, the videotape that had been shown to Cynthia on her first night in the toy box was found. Police knew they had to find the woman shown on the tape, and remarkably, they were able to. Her name was Kelly Garrett, who had been a newlywed for only days when she was kidnapped. When interviewed, Kelly claimed she had been abducted by Ray and a female she identified as Jesse Ray, who was Ray's daughter.

Like the other two women, Kelly had endured three days of rape and torture. She was then drugged and abandoned on the side of the road, close to where her new in-laws lived. Initially Kelly couldn't remember what had happened, and her in-laws assumed she had been binging on drugs and told her to leave. She went back to Colorado, and although she still had a degree of amnesia, she slowly started to remember the details of what had happened to her over time.

Trial and Judgment

Now that the police had three known victims, the decision was made to prosecute Ray in three trials. Each trial would be specific to an individual victim. The first trial, that of Cynthia's, ended in a mistrial, but when tried again, Ray was found guilty on the 12 counts of which he had been accused. The second trial was to be about Angelica's case, but unfortunately she passed away from pneumonia before it started, so this trial was abandoned. Before the third trial could be conducted, Ray decided to take a plea deal in exchange for a lighter sentence for his daughter, Jesse.

Ray was subsequently sentenced to 224 years for his crimes against these three women. It had taken two-and-a-half years for his trials to go ahead, and during this time Kelly Garrett had stated she hoped he would get life imprisonment because the death penalty was too easy for him. She wanted him to suffer, as they had suffered at his hands. During the police investigation, three accomplices were discovered and arrested and charged as well.

Through interviews and police work, a further victim was identified, Marie Parker, who had disappeared in 1997. Her body has never been found, and it has not been made clear how the police linked her to Ray, but an accomplice of his was charged with her murder. Dennis Roy Yancy had admitted to his wife that he had killed Marie by strangulation but was forced to do so, and his trial resulted in a conviction. He had taken a plea deal of twenty years, which had been offered because the prosecution knew it would be difficult to get a guilty verdict in the absence of a body and physical evidence. He was 28 years old at the time.

Yancy served eleven years in prison before being released on parole in 2011. However, he soon violated his probation and was returned to prison. He must now serve out the rest of his original sentence and will be unable to get parole until 2021.

Cynthia Lea Hendy, also known as 'Cindy', had been Ray's live-in girlfriend throughout his reign of terror on young women. But she had also been an accomplice, whether willing or enforced, and was tried and convicted of numerous kidnapping and accessory charges. She was sentenced to serve thirty-six years in prison; she avoided a life sentence by agreeing to cooperate with authorities in their search for more victims. According to Hendy, Ray had disposed of the bodies of his victims in the Elephant Butte reservoir, but despite thoroughly searching, no remains have ever been found.

Perhaps the most disturbing accomplice was Ray's own daughter Jesse. Formerly known as Glenda Jean Jesse Ray, she was subsequently arrested and charged with kidnapping, receiving a sentence of just two-and-a-half years plus five years' probation. Incredibly, Jesse had approached authorities back in 1986 claiming her father was involved in kidnapping and torturing women and then selling them as slaves to people in New Mexico. The FBI embarked on a year-long investigation into the accusations but were unable to locate or identify any victims. Despite intensive efforts, they could not find any evidence to suggest the accusations were true.

One has to wonder how a daughter could go from accusing her

father to the FBI of horrible acts to then assisting him with carrying out those same deeds.

Death and Aftermath

Ray was about to be interrogated by the state police in Lea County Correctional Facility when he suddenly suffered a heart attack and died. It was May 28, 2002, having barely started serving his sentence. Some may see his death as justice, but for his victims who wanted him to suffer the rest of his life in prison, they would have felt he had gotten off lightly. He had chained his victims up like a dog in a cage, and for many, seeing him locked in a small cell for the rest of his days would have been the equivalent.

During Ray's trials, each of the victims was given the opportunity to speak before his sentences were handed down. Kelly and Cynthia had sat hand in hand throughout the court process, often seen crying, reliving everything this monster had put them through. When it was time for Kelly to speak, she said she hoped he would be controlled, used and abused while in prison the same as he had done to them. She also declared she was a survivor, not a victim.

Angelica Montano's mother spoke on her behalf, having only recently lost her daughter to illness. Loretta Romero said her daughter had lost everything, including her smile, because of what Ray had done to her. Even the lives of Angelica's children had been ruined by Ray. Although Loretta claimed to have forgiven Ray, she stated she would never forget what he had done.

Bertha Vigil, Cynthia's grandmother, stood up to speak as well. Bertha told Ray he was a poor excuse for a human. She also asked if he would like it if she had done to his daughter what he had done to hers. According to Bertha, Cynthia suffered from nightmares each night, and Ray had ruined her life and her family's lives. She hoped he would burn in hell.

When it was Cynthia's turn to speak, her statements were perhaps the most emotional of them all. She believed no punishment given to Ray would ever be equal to the suffering she had endured. She was too scared to go out of the house on her own, was afraid of darkness, and terrified of feeling helpless or being tied down. Crying throughout her speech, she wanted Ray to spend his life inside the four walls of a cell and she hoped he would suffer just as she had.

David Parker Ray is suspected of killing up to sixty victims during the decades his toy box was in operation. The police were hoping he would give them more information regarding the identities of his victims and the location of their bodies, which was why he was meant to meet them on the day he suddenly died. Even his accomplices admitted he had killed a lot of women and had also murdered his business partner, but without further information, these claims can't be proven. More than 100 police officers searched Ray's home and the area surrounding it following his arrest, to no avail.

Transcripts from His Audio Tapes

Ray had made a series of audio tapes that he would play for his captives, and these would explain why the victim had been kidnapped and what was going to happen to her while being kept as a sex slave. The tapes were incredibly graphic, going into fine lurid detail about Ray's fantasies and what he liked to do to his slaves. They also carried a heavy warning about how the slave should behave to prevent even more suffering or even death.

Following are some excerpts from these terrifying audio tapes so you can see what these poor women had to endure from the minute they were chained inside the toy box.

Excerpts from Five Audio Tape Transcripts

"Hello there, bitch. Are you comfortable right now? I doubt it. Wrists and ankles chained. Gagged. Probably blindfolded. You are disoriented and scared, too, I would imagine. Perfectly normal, under the circumstances. For a little while, at least, you need to get your shit together and listen to this tape. It is very relevant to your situation. I'm going to tell you, in detail, why you have been kidnapped, what's going to happen to you and how long you'll be here. I don't know the details of your capture, because this tape is being created July 23rd, 1993, as a general advisory tape for future female captives. The information I'm going to give you is based on my experience dealing with captives over a period of several years. If, at a future date, there are any major changes in our procedures, the tape will be upgraded. Now, you are obviously here against your will, totally helpless, don't know where you're at, don't know what's gonna happen to you. You're very scared or very pissed off. I'm sure that you've already tried to get your wrists and ankles loose and know you can't. Now you're just waiting to see what's gonna happen next. You probably think you're gonna be raped and you're fuckin' sure right about that. Our primary interest is in what you've got between your legs. You'll be raped thoroughly and repeatedly, in every hole you've got. Because, basically, you've been snatched and brought here for us to train and use as a sex slave. Sound kind of far out? Well, I suppose it is to the uninitiated, but we do it all the time. It's gonna take a lot of adjustment on your part, and you're not gonna like it a fuckin' bit. But I don't give a big rat's ass about that. It's not like you're gonna have any choice about the matter. You've been taken by force, and you're going to be kept and used by force. What all this amounts to is that you're gonna be kept naked and chained up like an animal, to be used and abused any time we want to, any way that we want to. And you might as well start gettin' used to it, because you're gonna be kept here and used until such time as we get tired of fuckin' around with you . And we will, eventually, in a month or two, maybe three. It's no big deal. My lady friend and I have been keeping sex slaves for years. We both have kinky hang-ups involving rape, dungeon games, etc. We've found that it is extremely convenient to keep one or two female captives available constantly to, uh, satisfy our particular needs. We are very selective when we snatch a girl to use for these purposes.

I get off on mind games. After we get completely through with

15

you, you're gonna be drugged up real heavy, with a combination of sodium pentothal and phenobarbital. They are both hypnotic drugs that will make you extremely susceptible to hypnosis, autohypnosis, and hypnotic suggestion. You're gonna be kept drugged a couple of days, while I play with your mind. By the time I get through brainwashing you, you're not gonna remember a f*ckin' thing about this little adventure.

Here, your status is no more than that of one of the dogs, or of one of the animals out in the barn. Your only value to us is the fact that you have an attractive, usable body. And, like the rest of our animals, you will be fed and watered, kept in good physical condition, kept reasonably clean and allowed to use the toilet when necessary. In return, you're gonna be used hard, especially during your first few days while you're new and fresh. You're gonna be kept chained in a variety of different positions, usually with your legs or knees forced wide apart."

Consequently, you are gonna be kept in an environment that is even more secure than a prison cell. If it has not already been done, very shortly a steel collar is going to be padlocked around your neck. It has a long, heavy chain that is padlocked to a ring in the floor. The collar will never be removed, until you are turned loose. It's a permanent fixture. The hidden playroom, where you're gonna be kept, has steel walls, floor and ceiling. It is virtually soundproof and has a steel door with two keyed locks. The hinges are welded on and there are two heavy deadbolts on the outside. The room is totally escape proof, even with tools. Anytime that you are left unattended in the room, your wrists will be chained and there are electronic sensors to, uh, let us know if you move around too much. And if that's not enough, there is a closed-circuit TV system with a surveillance camera. It's wired to the main TV in the living room so we can check you once in a while or just set and watch you for the fun of it. Electronics is a wonderful thing. Expensive, but hell, everything in the room is expensive, and damn well worth it. If everybody knew how much fun it was to keep a sex slave, half the women would be chained up in somebody's basement."

You are a slave. You don't realize it yet, but you will eventually. I'm your master and the lady is your mistress. You will be totally docile. You'll be very quiet and you'll speak only when spoken to. Never initiate conversation. Keep your mouth shut. Any time that you are spoken to, you will be required to respond and it will be with proper speech. Remember that we are in the dungeon game and as long as you are here, it's the only game in town. Any time that you are asked a question where a yes or no answer is required, you will respond by saying, "yes, master; no, mistress; no, master; etcetera." You will show proper respect. Having to use the word master or mistress may sound funny, petty or vain to you, but that's all right. If you choose not to do it, you can laugh while you're being whipped or when your body is convulsing under the electroshock machine. You will respond to commands without protest or resistance. Do exactly what you're told, nothing else.

Remember that here you are a slave and failure to respond to a command will definitely get you in trouble.

Well, I believe I've told you about everything that I can. I cannot predict the future. I can't predict changes of procedure. But if this tape is being played for you, I have to assume that it is still reasonably accurate. And I can only give you advice. Be smart and be a survivor. Don't ever scream. Don't talk without permission. Be very quiet. Be docile and obedient and, by all means, show proper respect.

Have a nice day."

Seeking Ultimate Control

Although there have been other cases of women being kept as sex slaves, what David Parker Ray did to his victims is perhaps the most sadistic. He didn't just control his victims by inflicting physical terror; he also put them in an environment of constant psychological fear. For Ray it wasn't just about inflicting pain or fulfilling his sexual desires - he wanted to control his slaves completely by terrorizing them to the point where they would not try to leave.

Ray had spent many years planning, plotting and saving to create a space where he could do whatever he wanted to women without being caught. His so-called 'toy box' was filled with everything he could think of that would inflict pain. There was also evidence that Ray had researched some of his torture tools, to the point where he created diagrams to remind himself, and to terrorize his victims, of where on the body he could make them hurt the most.

When looking at the murders and horrendous assaults Ray committed, you soon realize that he also had control over the women who were in his life. His girlfriend of many years was a willing assistant to the kidnappings, and most likely played a part in at least some of the sexual assaults and torture sessions. Was she terrified of Ray herself? As it was, when his final victim made her break for freedom, Cindy fought tooth and nail to try and stop her from getting away. Was this loyalty to her man or was she frightened of receiving the same treatment?

Ray also had some level of control over his daughter Jesse. Here was a girl who previously had tried to get her own father arrested because she suspected he was involved in the slavery trade. She had gone all the way to the top with her information, to the FBI. Jesse wanted her father arrested and locked up for what she believed he was doing. But, the FBI failed to find any evidence and the report was forgotten.

Yet Jesse would later help her father commit his awful crimes. Although most daughters are daddy's girls and would do anything or their fathers, what Jesse did for Ray is unthinkable. And for a father to involve his daughter in his sick and twisted behaviors is deplorable. Did he have something over Jesse to force her to help him? Or was she too under his control just as his slaves had been? Perhaps, and most disturbingly, she too had the same urges and desires as her father. Even worse, maybe after the FBI failed to arrest her father the first time she came to think that rather than fight it, she should just accept her father's behavior.

Media

Film:

The Toy Box (2010)

Book:

Slow Death – James Fielder (2003)

CHAPTER 2:
James Huberty
– The McDonald's Massacre

On the morning of July 18, 1984, James Oliver Huberty kissed his wife Etna goodbye and stated he was 'off to hunt humans'. Despite such an ominous statement and his background history, Etna did nothing, and what followed would be one of the most devastating shooting rampages in modern American history. Huberty would take the lives of 21 innocent people and leave 19 others with horrifying injuries at a McDonald's restaurant in San Ysidro, San Diego.

An Ordinary Man

Huberty was born in 1942 in Canton, Ohio, and although he contracted the disease polio at just 3 years of age, he recovered well, albeit for some difficulties in walking. His father decided to purchase a farm in the 1950s, but because it was located in Amish country in Pennsylvania, Huberty's mother refused to move there. So while the family moved to the farm, his mother took off and became a sidewalk Southern Baptist preacher.

Huberty enrolled in sociology studies at Malone College in 1962, but he decided to change his studies and shifted to the Pittsburgh Institute of Mortuary Science in Pennsylvania. Here he would obtain his embalming license and would spend two years working in a funeral home. During his studies, he met Etna Markland and they married before Huberty had finished his mortuary license. Following his work in the funeral home, Huberty decided he wanted to become a welder, and the couple moved to Massillon in Ohio. They would subsequently have two daughters, Zelia and Cassandra, born in 1972 and 1974.

The home wasn't a happy one, with multiple reports and historical accounts of domestic violence. At one point, Etna notified the Canton Department of Children and Family Services that Huberty had 'messed up her jaw'. Despite this, there was no move by the authorities to remove the children, and Huberty was never charged with domestic assault. Etna claimed that when Huberty flew into one of his rages, she would pull out her tarot cards and pretend that she was reading his future. According to Etna, this would calm him down and pacify him.

Huberty developed very firm beliefs about society and the government, and he proclaimed to be a survivalist. He believed there was 'growing trouble' in the US and that businesses were failing because of the government's actions. He also believed the Federal Reserve System was being manipulated by international bankers in an attempt to send the country into bankruptcy.

Huberty claimed society was breaking down, possibly because of the Russians, and there was likely to be either a nuclear war or economic collapse.

To protect himself and his family, Huberty stocked up on non-perishable foods and weapons, allegedly spending thousands of dollars to make sure they would survive whatever was coming next. He apparently had so many guns in the house that he could reach one from wherever he happened to be sitting or standing in the house. All of his guns were kept loaded so he could be fully prepared to protect his family at any time.

In October 1983, Huberty packed up his family and shifted them to Tijuana in Mexico. Almost all of their possessions were placed in storage before they moved, except for the weapons and ammunition. He made sure he took those with him, just in case. While his children and wife were happy in Tijuana, Huberty was not, and they moved again within three months, this time locating to San Ysidro in San Diego.

Huberty was able to get a job as a security guard, and the family moved again from their new apartment to another, which happened to be just one block away from the McDonald's restaurant. After so many ups and downs for the family, things were going well for them until Huberty lost his job on July 10, 1984. This event would be the catalyst for what was about to occur next.

A Devastating Rampage

According to Huberty's wife, on July 15 he stated he thought he might have a mental health problem. On July 17 Huberty called a mental health clinic and asked for an appointment, and was told by the receptionist he would receive a call within a few hours. He gave them his contact details and waited, but the call never came. After several hours, Huberty went for a ride on his motorcycle. It would later be discovered that the receptionist Huberty had spoken to not only wrote his name down incorrectly, she also didn't think it was a crisis situation because he sounded calm and polite on the phone. It was therefore logged as a non-urgent matter which can take up to 48 hours before a call is returned.

About an hour after Huberty went for his ride, he came back home and he seemed to be in a contented frame of mind. The family ate dinner, then went for a bicycle ride together to a local park. Then Huberty and Etna sat and watched a movie after the children had gone to bed. Etna had no reason to be concerned at this point, because Huberty seemed to be calm and there were no signs of anger or aggression.

The morning of July 18, the family went to the San Diego zoo, and while they were walking, Huberty told Etna his life was over. Because he hadn't received a call from the mental health clinic, he said to his wife that 'society had their chance'. After the zoo, the family went to the nearby McDonald's for lunch, and then headed home. Not long after, Etna was relaxing on the bed when Huberty came in and leaned towards her saying that he wanted to kiss her goodbye. She asked Huberty where he was going, and he replied that he was 'going hunting humans'. As he left the house, he told his eldest daughter goodbye, saying he wouldn't be back.

Just before 4 pm, Huberty drove into the McDonald's carpark that was only 200 meters from his home. He was carrying an arsenal of guns and ammunition, including a 9mm Uzi carbine, a Browning semi-automatic pistol and a Winchester 12-gauge pump action shotgun. At the time he entered the restaurant, there were 45 people inside, including the staff. Straight away he pointed the shotgun at an employee, John Arnold, and the assistant manager Guillermo Flores shouted to Arnold to warn him. However, when Huberty tried to fire the gun it failed, and as he fiddled with it, Arnold thought it was a bad joke and started to walk away.

Neva Caine, the 22-year old manager, walked towards Arnold when Huberty suddenly fired a shot into the ceiling, then aimed his Uzi at Caine and shot her. He was struck underneath her eye and died within minutes. He then took aim at Arnold, shooting him in the chest and shouted for everyone to get on the ground. He called everyone dirty swine, and claimed to have killed thousands of people and was planning on killing another thousand. One of the customers, Victor Rivera, tried to reason with Huberty to get him to stop shooting, but Huberty responded by firing 14 bullets into him.

The majority of the customers tried to seek shelter underneath the tables and booths, and Huberty noticed a group of women and children huddled up together. Firing on the group, he killed Maria Colmenero-Silva and Claudia Perez, and wounded Imelda Perez and Aurora Peña. Pregnant Jackie Reyes was shot and killed, and when her 8-month old baby Carlos cried beside her, Huberty used his pistol and fired a single fatal shot into the baby's back.

The next victim was Laurence Versluis, a 62-year old man who was killed, and Huberty then noticed a family hiding beneath tables near the play area. Ronald Herrera was shielding Keith Thomas under a booth, and his wife Blythe Regan was using her body to shield their son Mateo beneath another. As Huberty walked towards the family, he continued to fire at those who were still seated. He then shot and wounded Thomas twice and shot Ronald eight times, but remarkably he survived. His wife and son, however, were not as fortunate, and both Blythe and Mateo were shot in the head numerous times.

Arisdelsi Vuelvas Vargas was shielding her friend Guadalupe del Rio beneath a booth when Huberty approached them. Vargas was shot just once in the back of the head, which did not kill her straight away. In fact, she made it to the hospital but succumbed to her injury the following day. Del Rio, despite being shot multiple times, survived the attack. Hugo Velazquez Vasquez, a 45-year-old banker, was shot and killed while sitting at another booth.

Multiple calls were made to the emergency services, with the first arriving at 4 pm. However, the dispatcher sent the officers to the wrong McDonald's which was two miles away. It took approximately ten minutes for police to arrive at the right restaurant, and they quickly locked down a six-block radius of the area. A command post was set up and 175 officers were sent to the scene. Within an hour, the SWAT team arrived.

Not long after the first emergency call was made, Lydia Flores drove her car into the parking lot and pulled up by the window where food is picked up. She noticed the windows were shattered, then heard the sounds of gunfire. Flores quickly reversed back, stopping only when her car hit a fence. She then hid with her 2-year old daughter until the shooting had stopped.

Meanwhile, three young boys out for a bike ride rode up to the restaurant to buy some drinks. A person across the road was yelling out to the boys to warn them, but they couldn't hear what was being said. Confused, the boys hesitated, and having been seen by Huberty, he opened fire on them. Joshua Coleman was shot in the arm, leg and back, and fell to the ground. Omar Alonso Hernandez had been shot in the back multiple times, and David Flores Delgardo was shot in the head numerous times. Both Hernandez and Delgardo died, and Coleman remembered looking over at them on the ground and vomiting at the sight.

The next victims shot were elderly couple Miguel Victoria Ulloa who was 74, and his wife Aida Velazquez Victoria, 69. They were walking towards the restaurant, and as Miguel reached for the door, Huberty shot Aida in the face with the shotgun, killing her, and Miguel was wounded. He sat on the ground cradling Aida and wiping the blood off her face, shouting and cursing at Huberty who then walked up to Miguel and shot him in the head, killing him.

At around 4:10 pm, Mexicans Astolfo Felix and his wife Maricela were driving towards the restaurant with their 4-month-old daughter Karlita in the car. They had noticed the broken window, and thought the man walking towards them was there to fix it. But the man was Huberty, and he fired both the Uzi and the shotgun at the family. Astolfo was shot in the head and the chest, and Maricela was hit in the face, chest and arms, leaving her alive but blind in one eye and unable to use a hand. The baby, Karlita, was shot in the chest, neck and abdomen, and as Astolfo and Maricela staggered away from the car and Huberty, Maricela passed her baby to a woman who was running away and begged her to save her baby. Incredibly, all three of the Felix family survived their injuries.

Witnesses who survived the rampage later recalled seeing Huberty approach the service counter and adjust the channel on a radio. It's possible he was looking to see if there were any news reports. He tuned the radio to a music channel, then proceeded to continue on his mission to shoot everyone in the restaurant. He then entered the kitchen area and found six employees hiding. Paulina López, Elsa Borboa-Fierro and Margarita Padilla were all killed. Alberto Leos was wounded, having been shot multiple times, and managed to flee to the basement utility room to hide with four other employees and a customer.

At one point, Huberty noticed a fire engine drive close by, and he fired on it multiple times. However, although the vehicle was struck by many bullets, nobody was hurt or killed inside the fire engine. He then noticed one of the teenagers he had shot, Jose Pérez was moaning and Huberty proceeded to shoot him in the head, killing him instantly. Next to Pérez, his neighbor and friend Gloria González was shot and killed, as was Michelle Carncross. There was a slight lull in the shooting at one point, and Aurora Péna took a chance and opened her eyes to see what was going on. Terrifyingly, Huberty was staring right back at her, and angry she was still alive, he threw a packet of fries at her, then shot her again in the chest, neck and arm. Although her recovery would prove to be prolonged, she did survive her injuries.

At first police couldn't ascertain how many shooters were actually inside the restaurant. Because Huberty was using a variety of weapons, it wasn't clear if there was more than one shooter. The light reflecting on the shattered panels of the windows obscured what was happening inside, and it was incredibly difficult for police to work out what to do. The SWAT team placed a sniper on top of the building next door and instructed him to shoot to kill if he was able to get a clear shot at the gunman.

That opportunity presented itself at 5:17 pm, when Huberty moved directly into the sniper's sights. A single round was fired from the sniper's weapon striking Huberty in the chest. The bullet severed the aorta and exited out his spine, knocking him backwards on to the floor. The aorta is the biggest artery in the body, so it only took seconds for Huberty to take his last breath and die on the floor in front of the counter.

The entire rampage had gone on for 78 minutes. It is estimated Huberty fired at least 245 rounds of ammunition on his victims ranging in age from 8 months to 74 years. The majority of the victims were of Mexican or Mexican-American descent, but this doesn't mean it was a racial attack. It was simply due to local demographics of the area.

A Multitude of Victims

Those killed inside the restaurant:

Neva Denise Caine – aged 22 – (Manager of the McDonald's) shot in the face

Elsa Herlinda Borboa-Fierro – aged 19 – (employee)

Maria Elena Colmenero-Silva – aged 19 – shot in the chest

Michelle Deanne Carncross – aged 18

Gloria López González – aged 22

Mateo Herrera – aged 11 – (Blythe Herrera's son) multiple gunshots to the head

Blythe Regan Herrera – aged 31 – multiple gunshots to the head

Margarita Padilla – aged 18 – (employee)

Paulina Aquino López – aged 21 – (employee)

Jose Rubén Lozano Perez – aged 19

Claudia Perez – aged 9 – shot in the head, cheek, armpit, hip, torso and thigh

Jackie Lynn Wright Reyes – aged 18 – received 48 gunshot wounds

Carlos Reyes – aged 8 months – single shot to the back

Victor Maximillian Rivera – aged 25 – shot 14 times

Hugo Luis Velazquez Vasquez – aged 45 – shot in the chest

Laurence Herman Versluis – aged 62

Arisdelsi Vuelvas Vargas – aged 31 – shot in the head

Killed outside:

Omar Alonso Hernandez – aged 11 – shot in the body and the head

David Flores Delgado – aged 11 – shot in the body and the head

Aida Velazquez Victoria – aged 69 – shot in the face

Miguel Victoria Ulloa – aged 74 – shot in the head

Injured but survived:

John Arnold – aged 16 – shot in the torso

Juan Acosta – aged 33

Astolfo Cejundo – aged 26

Anthony Atkins – aged 36

Guadalupe del Rio – aged 24 – received multiple gunshot wounds

Joshua Coleman – aged 11 – shot in the arms, hands, stomach and buttocks

Astolfo Felix – aged 31 – shot in the neck and chest

Maricela Felix – aged 23 – shot in the head, chest and arms

Karlita Felix – aged 4 months – shot in the torso and the head

Ronald Herrera – aged 33 – shot in the head, stomach, shoulder, arm and hip

Aurora Péna – aged 11 – shot in the neck, jaw, leg and arm

Alberto Leos – aged 17 – (employee)

Imelda Perez – aged 15

Francisco Lopez – aged 22

Mireya Rivera – aged 4

Maria Rivera – aged 25

Keith Thomas – aged 12 – shot in the arm and shoulder

Kenneth Villegas – aged 22

Juan Tokano – aged 33

Why?

When an incident as devastating and seemingly irrational takes place, the number one question is always why? For a man to walk into what is unquestionably a kid-friendly and family-oriented restaurant and just open fire on every single person inside is incomprehensible for the majority of the population. And yet this wasn't the first time such an atrocity had happened, and unfortunately, it is not likely to be the last.

During the aftermath Huberty, his family and his life were analyzed from all directions in the search for answers. Huberty and his wife Etna were very well known by the police and not for the right reason either. There had been numerous complaints placed against the couple by neighbors for noise, vicious guard dogs and violence within the home. Etna herself had previously been arrested for threatening a woman with a pistol. She had even encouraged her daughter Zelia to assault another child. Despite all the complaints and the known domestic violence in the home, Huberty had only ever been arrested once, and that was for being drunk and disorderly.

The results of Huberty's autopsy ruled out any evidence of alcohol or drugs in his system, so there was no chemical cause for his behavior. However, his body did contain high levels of metals, particularly cadmium and lead. This was most likely the result of fumes he inhaled while working for Babcock and Wilcox as a welder for 14 years. Whether these high levels could have caused Huberty to go out and shoot people is unproven.

His mental health had to be brought into question, especially since he himself had tried to get some help just three days before the massacre took place. His wife later stated that he would complain of hearing voices, especially in the months leading up to that dreadful day. If the mental health clinic had called back that day, perhaps he could have been treated and medicated if necessary, but unfortunately it is debatable as to whether that still would have prevented the tragedy from occurring.

Many of Huberty's former co-workers and associates remembered Huberty as being quite obsessed with guns and would often make claims of one day shooting people. Terry Kelly worked with him at Babcock & Wilcox, and he claimed Huberty was always talking about shooting somebody. When Huberty lost his job there, he stated that if it was the end of him being able to provide for his family he would take everyone else with him.

Brother Dave Lombardi, a minister of the Trinity Gospel Temple in Canton, had married Huberty and Etna and knew them both very well. He believed Huberty's problems were the product of his childhood, especially once his mother abandoned the family. Apparently, Huberty's father went on to marry a young teacher who had her own children as well. Huberty did not get along with his new stepmother, and a neighbor claimed that when Huberty came home he would fire several shots in to the air to let them know he was there. This certainly isn't normal behavior.

As for the location Huberty chose for his rampage, there is much speculation about his reasons for selecting the McDonald's restaurant and whether it has any bearing on what went on that day. One of the theories was that it was because the restaurant faced towards Tijuana, the Mexican border town, and Huberty was known to have a dislike of Hispanics. He believed they came and took away the jobs that men like himself could have had. He also didn't like the way they were so comfortable in McDonald's, which he considered to be a 'white middle-class restaurant'. Essentially he didn't think they had the right to be there.

Another theory is that being so close to the border, it was a popular stop for American tourists returning from day trips to Tijuana. From there they would head off down the freeways to places like California, back to their happy and good lives, which

Huberty resented because his own was so miserable. Or perhaps it was because McDonald's advertising peddled the idea of a wonderful family life filled with laughter and happiness, and that this dream world was completely opposite to what Huberty had experienced in his own life.

So, was Huberty a sick and twisted individual shaped by his seemingly unhappy childhood? Can a parental divorce really create such darkness in a child's mind? Generally, no. If he had suffered horrible abuse or had a childhood full of tragedy, then perhaps it could be blamed on that. But for all intents and purposes, it seems his childhood was no different than millions of other children, and they don't all grow up and become spree killers.

The mental health suggestion is perhaps the most likely reason for Huberty going on his murderous rampage that day. He had been talking about shooting people for years, and although there is no evidence he had ever done so previously, that thought was obviously never far from his mind. Huberty was a dark and miserable loner, and this is commonly seen in spree killers. For him to have sought help just days earlier indicates he knew that he was very unwell. Being rejected in his mind by not receiving the call for an appointment was perhaps the final straw - the trigger that set everything in motion.

Whatever his reasons, Huberty had obviously put some level of planning and thought into what he was going to do. He had chosen the location, packed his bag with all the ammunition he needed, kissed his wife goodbye and told his daughter he wouldn't be back. He knew that his mission would be a fatal one, and he did it all very calmly. His daughter would later say that if she had known what her father was about to do that day she would have killed him herself.

The Aftermath

In the immediate aftermath, there were so many victims that the local funeral homes couldn't cope. Instead, all of the wakes were held at the Civic Center, and the Mount Carmel Church conducted back-to-back funeral masses. Huberty himself was cremated on July 23, 1984, and the ashes interred in Ohio. His wife Etna and her two daughters moved to Spring Valley and the children took on false names to protect their identity. Sadly Etna passed away in 2003 of breast cancer.

Incredibly, the restaurant itself had been completely renovated and rebuilt within two days of the shootings. McDonald's had planned to reopen as soon as possible, but following discussion with the leaders of the community, it was decided it would never reopen on that site. Despite the money put into repairing the building, it was subsequently destroyed on July 28 and another restaurant was built nearby. A donation of $1 million was made to the survivor's fund on behalf of the company.

The ground where the restaurant had once stood was given to the city with the proviso that another restaurant could never be built there. For more than four years, the community debated over a variety plans to create a memorial on the site. Some people had erected makeshift memorials but these were taken down. Eventually in 1988, the land was sold to nearby Southwestern College and an agreement was made that a large area in the front would be used to create a permanent memorial to those who had died.

The final design of the memorial involves 21 hexagonal white marble pillars, one for each victim. They range in heights to show the difference in ages and race of the victims. Each pillar has a victim's name on it and they are bonded together as a symbol of the community coming together at times of tragedy. Every year on the anniversary of the rampage, flowers are laid at the memorial. On November 1, the Mexican Day of the Dead, offerings and candles are placed on behalf of those who died that day.

Huberty's deadly rampage had an immediate aftereffect on the San Diego police force. They immediately increased the training for the special units, and better firearms were purchased. At the time, most of the officers who responded to the scene were only equipped with .38 pistols, which were no match for the Uzi and shotgun Huberty was carrying. The procedures and policies put in place after the tragedy resulted in a better trained and better-armed team that are able to respond quickly and at any time they are needed.

Many of the families who lost loved ones, and those who had

survived, sued the McDonald's Corporation and the local franchise holder in the Superior Court. The court dismissed these lawsuits before trial, but the families appealed the decision. The Court of Appeal held up the dismissal on July 25, 1987, stating that the company was not responsible for the actions of a madman, and the lawsuits could not prove the restaurant was to blame because they did not have security guards. It was determined that there was nothing McDonald's could have done to deter Huberty as he was prepared to die that day.

Despite not being in the restaurant that day, Huberty's wife was the first person to receive a payout from the survivor's fund, which seems ludicrous. Many of the local residents protested this, unsurprisingly. She later tried to sue Babcock & Wilcox for $5 million claiming the metal fumes Huberty had inhaled for so many years had caused him to suffer delusions and rage. She also attempted to sue McDonald's, claiming that their food resulted in Huberty having a poor diet, and when combined with the 'high metal poisoning', this too contributed to his disturbed state of mind. Of course both cases were unsuccessful and were dismissed.

It seems inconceivable that Etna would try to make money out of the situation, after what her husband had done to so many families. Many of the survivors were left with lifelong disabilities and massive medical bills, and if anyone deserved a payout, it was them. Etna may not have predicted her husband was going to do something so horrendous, but the warning signs that something was very wrong were certainly there. Although it is tragic that her children lost their father and she lost her husband, it occurred because of his own actions. The others were simply sitting in a family restaurant having something to eat when Huberty walked through the door that day.

Survivor Stories

Often when a tragedy like this occurs, the focus is on the dead, rather than those who survived, some of who endure a lifetime of pain, suffering and mental anguish because of the injuries they endured, the sights they were forced to see, or the paralyzing fear of being helpless in such a deadly situation. Here are the stories of some of those who survived James Huberty's rampage.

Karla (Karlita) Felix

Karla was just a baby, 4 months old, on the day Huberty went on a shooting rampage. She was being held in her mother's arms as she exited their car, trying desperately to escape the gunman's bullets. Her mother was shot in the eye and in the stomach. Her father also suffered gunshot wounds. And baby Karla was shot in the head. Her parents pushed her into the arms of a stranger, begging for help for their baby daughter, and she was then passed on to a policeman and rushed to the nearest hospital.

Although she was just a baby at the time, the anniversary of the tragedy always strikes a chord in Karla, and she spends that day watching the videos of that day. She finds it hard to believe that not only was she involved, but that she was shot in the head and survived it. For a baby to survive a wound like that is truly miraculous. As well as some scars on her back, there is still half a bullet lodged in her head that will always remain there.

Joshua Coleman

Perhaps one of the most tragic photographs taken on that day was the one showing three young boys lying on the sidewalk outside the restaurant, their bicycles at their feet. Two of those boys were killed right there, and one survived – Joshua Coleman. Although many of the survivors remain haunted by what happened, Joshua doesn't believe he is one of them.

He remembers his friends and what happened to them every anniversary, but he does not feel sorry for himself. He claims that he is not bothered by death, and he does not let what occurred stop him from living his life. His memory of that day is still very strong, and he recalls how he and his friends, Omar Hernandez and David Flores, had ridden their bicycles to the store to buy doughnuts. Joshua had wanted some ice cream as well, so they walked their bicycles over to the McDonald's restaurant.

As they walked along the sidewalk, Joshua heard many yell out, and when he turned to see who it was, he was shot in the side. His friends were shot also, and as he lay on the hot ground, the idea to play dead entered his mind, and that's exactly what he did.

After the incident, Joshua was moved to another school to avoid him being scrutinized by others, and he received hundreds of letters of sympathy and support from strangers. Joshua has never seen a therapist to help him deal with the trauma of the massacre. He never thought he needed it, and still doesn't, and his parents didn't think it was necessary either.

Ken Dickey

Ken was 20 years old at the time and worked behind the counter at McDonald's while he studied at college. When Huberty started shooting, Ken and another co-worker fled downstairs to the utility room in the basement. They would eventually be joined by three female workers, a woman with a baby and a man who was bleeding from his injuries. There they stayed until police came and knocked on the door. There were still fearful, but opened the door anyway.

As they were taken through the restaurant, police instructed them to place a hand on the shoulder of the person in front of them and only look at the wall on the left. This was to protect them from seeing the horrific scene of dead bodies, but Ken does remember seeing some blood spatters. For many days afterwards, Ken would sit in a chair for long periods of time and wonder what he could have done to help save those who were killed. He felt that instead of doing what a hero would have, he ran away in fear to save himself.

Nowadays he is married with a young child and lives in Payette, Idaho. He also teaches chemistry at the high school. The only times he ever returns to San Diego is to see his parents. Although he can sometimes go without thinking of that terrible day for four or five months at a time, those memories always return at some point.

Aurora Péna-Rivera

At the time of the shooting, Aurora was just 11 years old and was at McDonald's with a group of friends and family. They were standing at the service counter when Huberty entered, and of the group of six, four were killed. Aurora was lying on the floor with her eyes tightly closed, completely in fear. But, curiosity got the better of her, and thinking the gunman was a long way away, she opened her eyes. He was looking right at her. He picked up his gun and shot her. Bullets struck her in the jaw and the legs.

For a very long time, Aurora couldn't talk about what happened at all. The sounds, the sights, the dead and dying all around her, were too much for her to voice out loud. One day she was at another restaurant and an intoxicated man started yelling, and she immediately broke down. It had brought back all those memories of that terrible man who had brought tragedy upon them all.

At first she attended therapy but found that it made things a lot worse. She told her mother she didn't want to see any more doctors and her mother agreed. Instead she learned to accept what had happened and all the feelings associated with it such as loss and guilt.

Aurora now works for the Navy as an administrative assistant and is the mother of a young girl. Children often ask her about the scars she has on her leg which sometimes annoys her. Sometimes she just tells them she had a fall. Every now and then, she runs into Adelina Hernandez, whose son Omar was shot and killed outside the restaurant while with Joshua Coleman.

Adelina works at the local Elementary school so she can still surround herself with children. Omar had attended that same school, and being there and with the kids reminds her of him. To her it is like therapy or medicine. She doesn't get depressed anymore, only on rare occasions, and it is at this time she plays a cassette tape they had made when Omar was 9 years old.

Was It Preventable?

There are always investigations and discussions after a murderous rampage like that of James Huberty takes place. Hindsight is an incredible thing, and the first question always asked is whether or not it could have been prevented. Clearly Huberty was not of sound mind for a period of time leading up to that dreadful day, but was he actually insane? Or was Huberty just fed up with the world and what he perceived the government and major corporations were guilty of?

An insane man doesn't plan his actions ahead of time - they are almost always random and on the spur of the moment. There is evidence that Huberty had at least put some thought into planning his attack, by the way he had chosen the location, ensured he had enough ammunition and weapons on him, and said goodbye to his family. The trip to the zoo that morning was most likely his way of trying to leave his children with a happy memory of that day.

The fact that Huberty himself had called a mental health clinic just three days beforehand shows that he was sane enough to know he needed help. Even his wife claimed later that he had been mentally deteriorating for quite some time, yet she did nothing to seek help for her husband. The home life was miserable, with frequent arguments and bouts of violence, most likely on both sides considering she had been arrested previously for pointing a gun at someone.

It is impossible to ignore the possibility that if Huberty had been seen by the mental health clinic that day, this nightmare could have been prevented. He may have been admitted to a hospital, placed on medication, and supervised as he recovered from whatever mental illness he was plagued with. He was asking for help and couldn't get it, which was truly tragic. The final rejection he would have felt when the clinic didn't call him back would have been the final straw. His head was full of these dark and murderous thoughts and it seemed nobody was going to help him.

However, the blame must still lie entirely with Huberty. He was the one that walked into the McDonald's restaurant that day armed to the hilt and opened fire. Nobody made him do it, and even those who hear voices can usually ignore them. Huberty was full of hatred, disappointment and unhappiness. He chose a place that to the majority of people represents happiness and family. A restaurant full of innocent families, friends and coworkers, enjoying their lunch, and he ruthlessly opened fire on everyone in there regardless of age, gender or ethnicity. He didn't care who he killed, or who would be affected by their deaths.

James Huberty was obviously a sick man, and there are plenty of 'what ifs' that are left unanswered. What if the clinic had called back; what if his wife had pushed for him to get help; what if people in his life had paid more attention to what he said. But, even though you can look back, you can't go back and change anything.

Media

Film:

77 Minutes - (2016)

CHAPTER 3:
Fritz Haarmann
– The Butcher of Hanover

Friedrich Heinrich Karl Haarmann, commonly referred to as 'Fritz', was also known as The Butcher of Hanover, the Vampire of Hanover and the Wolf Man. These names were given because of the manner in which Fritz Haarmann murdered, dismembered and disposed of the young men he lured back to his apartment. It is believed Haarmann was responsible for at least 27 murders between 1918 and 1924 in Hanover, Germany, and his level of depravity and arrogance was astounding.

An Effeminate Child

Haarmann was born in 1879, the youngest of six children to Ollie and Johanna Haarmann. The children received very little attention from their father, and Haarmann was said to be spoilt by his mother. Johanna was seven years older than Ollie, and many believed he married her for her money, and he was known to indulge in many affairs throughout their marriage. Ollie was short-tempered and could be very argumentative, and Haarmann allegedly developed a strong hatred of his father which lasted until he died in 1921.

As a child, Haarmann was quiet and didn't socialize with other children. He had a few friends but he mostly played with his siblings when he wasn't at school. He steered clear of the usual boys' games and activities and preferred to dress up in his sisters' clothes and play with their dolls. Haarmann was very well behaved at school but struggled academically and twice was made to repeat a year. He was apparently molested by a teacher when he was only 8 years old, but he never discussed this with anyone in detail.

Although he displayed effeminate traits, Haarmann developed into a fit and strong young man. He left school in 1894 and worked briefly as a locksmith apprentice until he enrolled in the military academy at the age of 15. The academy was located in Breisach, and he started his training on April 4, 1895. He adapted well to being in the military, but five months into his service, he started to suffer from spells where he would lose consciousness. These episodes were diagnosed as epilepsy and he subsequently self-discharged from the military.

On his return to Hanover, Haarmann worked for his father in his cigar factory for a short period. Within months of his return, Haarmann began committing his first sexual offenses against young boys in the area. He would lure them to areas that were secluded, especially cellars, and then abuse them sexually. His first arrest for these offenses occurred in July 1896, and because he continued to commit these crimes, he was placed in a mental institution. He was deemed to be 'incurably deranged' by psychologist Gurt Schmalfuss and was declared unfit to stand trial. Haarmann was ordered to remain indefinitely at the mental institution.

However, seven months after being incarcerated at the institution, Haarmann managed to escape. It's believed his mother helped him, and he fled to Switzerland, staying there for 16 months before returning to Hanover. In 1900, he had met a woman called Erna Loewert and they became engaged, as she had fallen pregnant. She would later have an abortion. And in October that same year, Haarmann was called up for compulsory military service.

He was deployed to the city of Colmar and served in the Number 10 Rifle Battalion, and became regarded as a great marksman and an exemplary soldier. Haarmann himself would later refer to this time as being the happiest he had been. However, whilst on an exercise in October 1901, he suffered from dizzy spells and ended up in hospital for more than four months. It was then determined he was unfit to complete his military service and work and was given a medical discharge, which meant he would receive a military pension.

Haarmann returned to Hanover to live with his fiancée and worked briefly for his father again. Things did not go well, and at one point he filed a lawsuit against his father claiming he could not work due to his medical problems as stated by the military. His father contested and the charges were dropped. A year later, Haarmann and his father became embroiled in a violent fight, and this time it was his father who filed a lawsuit against him. He claimed Haarmann had made death threats towards him and that he should be returned to the mental institution. The charges were again dropped, but Haarmann was ordered to have a psychiatric examination. This time the doctor came to the conclusion that Haarmann was not mentally unstable but perhaps morally inferior.

Despite all the conflict between father and son, Haarmann received some money from his father to help him set up his own business as a fishmonger. He had tried to work as an insurance salesman, but in 1904 the military officially classified him as being unable to work due to disability. This led to an increase in his military pension. His fiancée ended their engagement that same year, despite being pregnant again. It is believed Haarmann had accused her of having an affair, and because the business had been placed in her name, she ordered Haarmann to leave.

Over the next ten years, Haarmann embarked on a criminal career that included being a con artist, burglar and petty thief. From time to time he was able to work legitimately, but he couldn't stop himself from stealing from the customers or his employers. In 1905 he began receiving prison sentences for crimes including assault, larceny and embezzlement. Although the sentences were generally short, he would still spend most of the period between 1905 and 1912 locked up in prison.

Haarmann did not stay out of prison for long, and was sent back there in the later months of 1913 following an arrest for burglary. A stash of stolen items was found in his home, and these had been linked back to other burglaries. Haarmann insisted he was innocent but was found guilty and sentenced to serve another five years in prison. Four years into his sentence and with World War I well underway, there was a shortage of domestic labor in Germany, largely because of compulsory conscription. Therefore, Haarmann was allowed to leave the prison during the day to do grounds work at nearby manor houses, and he would have to return each evening once he had finished work.

Once he had completed his sentence, Haarmann moved to Berlin for a short while, then returned to Hanover. He was astounded by the poverty that was now abundant following the loss of the War, and Haarmann again returned to a life of crime. He made several contacts at Hanover Central Station so he could trade any contraband property he could find. As it was, there was already a huge increase in crimes such as assault, theft and murder, and the black market was in full swing.

It was during this time that Haarmann began to create a relationship with the local police as an informer, predominantly so he could take their attention off him so he could continue his criminal acts. Also, by acting as an informant, Haarmann was free to roam around Hanover Station at will, which enabled him to come into contact with young boys. The police were well aware of Haarmann's criminal record and the fact he was a homosexual, which was illegal in those times, but because he was able to give them good information regarding other criminals, they allowed him to continue to act as an informant.

The Butcher of Hanover

Beginning in 1918, over the next six years, Haarmann is known to have murdered at least 24 victims, although the true number is likely to be 27. The victims were all boys or young men aged between 10 and 22, and most were teenagers. Haarmann would lure the boys back to one of his residences with the promise of accommodation, assistance or work, and sometimes he would even pretend to arrest them. Once inside, he would usually give them some food and something to drink, and then he would strike. Haarmann's method of murder was to bite the Adam's apple of his victims, something he referred to as a love bite, which would either asphyxiate the victim or on some occasions the bite would go right through the trachea.

Once dead, Haarmann would cut the bodies up and throw them in the Leine River, except for his very first victim who was buried, and his final victim who ended up in a lake near the Herrenhausen Gardens. Whatever possessions the victims had would be kept for Haarmann or his lover Hans Grans, and they would either wear them or sell them on the black market. Sometimes they would even give these items to friends as presents.

Haarmann was known to sell meat on the black market, often claiming it was horse or pork, and it was almost always cut up as minced meat. Whenever he was asked where the meat had come from, he would claim he got it from a butcher named Karl. However, these stories would change from time to time, and when police investigated, they couldn't confirm the existence of Karl. This led many to speculate following his arrest that perhaps the meat he was selling was human.

The first victim was 17-year-old Friedel Rothe, who had disappeared on September 27, 1918. He had been seen with Haarmann that same day. Rothe's family pressed the police to investigate Haarmann and they subsequently raided his apartment in October. When they entered the apartment there was a 13-year-old boy who was semi-naked in the room. Haarmann was arrested and charged with battery and sexual assault of a minor and received a 9-month sentence. However, he somehow managed to avoid serving his sentence until 1920.

In October 1919, Haarmann met a young runaway called Hans Grans who was just 18 years old, who had been sleeping near the station for about two weeks and was selling clothing at the station. Grans was actually a heterosexual, but he approached Haarmann with the intent of selling his body to him sexually, because he had heard from others that Haarmann was homosexual. Before long, Haarmann invited Grans to move into his apartment with him, and they would eventually become lovers and accomplices in the criminal world.

Haarmann was completely smitten with Grans, even though he was aware he was being manipulated. Every now and then, Haarmann would kick him out, then beg for him to come back. Haarmann ended up serving his earlier 9-month sentence starting in March 1920. Incredibly, when he was released, the police allowed him to once again be an informer. He lived with Grans in a hotel for a while, and then they moved in with a family until Haarmann heard of a vacant apartment in Neue Straβe beside the Leine River. The pair moved into their new home on July 1, 1921.

The next known victim was Fritz Franke, a 17-year-old pianist who had come into contact with Haarmann at Hanover Station. Franke was invited back to the apartment and introduced to Grans and two girls, one of whom was supposedly also Grans' lover. The girls left, and when they returned the next day they were told Franke had traveled on to Hamburg. It is uncertain how much Grans knew about this murder and whether or not he had any idea what Haarmann was planning to do with the young man. Haarmann, however, later claimed that Grans had come home unexpectedly and seen the naked body of Franke on Haarmann's bed. According to Haarmann Grans just looked at him and asked when he should come back.

Haarmann met 17-year-old Wilhelm Schulze at Hanover Station just five weeks after he had murdered Franke. Although his body was never found, it was presumed he had been murdered by Haarmann as his clothing was in the possession of Haarmann's landlady. Two further victims were murdered at this apartment before Haarmann and Grans left in June. Roland Huch was a 16-year-old who had told his friend he was running away to join the Marines but was never heard from again. Hans Sonnenfeld was a 19-year-old who had disappeared sometime around May 31, and Haarmann was seen wearing his overcoat after he had gone missing, which was a very distinctive yellow color.

Haarmann and Grans moved to an attic apartment at Rote Reihe, which was really just a single room. Only two weeks later, the neighbor's son, Ernst Ehrenberg, 13, went missing. He had been sent out to run an errand and never returned. Later his braces and cap would be found in Haarmann's room. On August 24, Heinrich Struβ an 18-year-old office clerk, disappeared and, again, his belongings would later be found in Haarmann's possession. A month later, Paul Bronischewski, 17, went missing while traveling to the city of Bochum. Inquiries by the police discovered he had gotten off the train at Hanover, where he happened to meet Haarmann. His trousers, jacket, knapsack and towel were all located in Haarmann's apartment.

Richard Gräf, 17, told his family that he had met a man at Hanover Station who claimed to have some work for him. He would subsequently be murdered around September 30, 1923. A fortnight later, Wilhelm Erdner did not make it home after work and was reported missing. His parents made inquiries and were made aware that their son had met a Detective Fritz Honnerbrock, which was a pseudonym used by Haarmann. With the 16-year-old's bicycle in their possession, Haarmann and Grans quickly sold it to get rid of it.

Just a week after selling the bicycle, Haarmann killed two more teenage boys. Hermann Wolf was just 15 years old when he went missing from Hanover Station on October 24, and 13-year-old Heinz Brinkmann was last seen at the station on October 27. Interestingly, Haarmann denied ever killing Hermann Wolf, and he was not convicted of his murder. On November 10, Adolf Hannappel, a 17- year-old carpentry apprentice went missing from Hanover Station. Several witnesses had seen him at the station and saw him walking towards a café with two men, later identified as Grans and Haarmann.

Adolf Hennies, 19, went missing on December 6 while out looking for employment. His remains were never found, and there was some dispute as to who had actually killed him. While Haarmann did admit to dismembering Hennies' body, he claimed he didn't kill him. He said he came home and found his body in the company of both Grans and another criminal called Hugo Wittkowski. Because the testimony regarding Hennies' murder was conflicting, neither Haarmann nor Grans were convicted of this murder.

By now Haarmann's killing was escalating rapidly. The time between each murder was getting shorter, yet there did not seem to be a shortage of victims. On January 5, 1924, 17-year-old Ernst Spiecker went missing. A friend of his would later testify that Spiecker and Haarmann had met before and knew each other. His possessions were found in Haarmann's house, and although he couldn't remember him, Haarmann said he would have to assume he was one of his victims.

Just ten days later, 20-year- old Heinrich Koch was killed by Haarmann. Again it is believed they knew each other previously. Two more victims were killed within the following month – Willi Senger, 19, and Hermann Speichert, 16. Then there was a break in the murders, and the next victim wasn't killed until around April 1. This victim was an acquaintance of Haarmann named Hermann Bock. His possessions were found in Haarmann's apartment following his arrest, and his suitcase had been given to Haarmann's landlady. Haarmann had also tried to persuade Bock's friends not to report him missing.

A week later a 16-year-old runaway called Alfred Hogrefe disappeared from Hanover Station. Then nine days later, Wilhelm Apel, 16, was murdered by Haarmann. It seemed the murders were escalating once more. Robert Witzel, 18, borrowed some money from his mother to go and see the circus and was never heard from again. His parents discovered their son had been seen with an 'official from the station' escorting him to the circus. Haarmann later confessed to the murder saying it had taken place that same night, and he had then dismembered his body and thrown it into the Leine River.

Two weeks later, 14-year-old Heinz Martin was murdered, his clothing later found in Haarmann's possession. On May 26, Fritz Wittig, a 17-year-old salesman was killed, allegedly because Grans wanted his suit. He too was dismembered and thrown in the river. That very same day, Haarmann killed Friedrich Abeling who was just 10 years old and believed to be Haarmann's youngest victim. A fortnight later, Haarmann murdered Friedrich Koch, 16, who had been walking to college. Witnesses saw Haarmann with Koch and would later testify at his trial.

The last victim to die at the hands of Haarmann was 17-year-old Erich de Vries. On June 14, De Vries had come into contact with Haarmann at Hanover Station. Following his murder, his dismembered body was placed in a bag that had belonged to Friedrich Koch and thrown into the lake at the entrance of Herrenhausen Gardens. Haarmann said after his arrest that it had taken him four trips to carry all the remains of Koch there.

Capture and Confession

A human skull was found near the Leine River by two children on May 17, 1924. The skull bore evidence of knife wounds and appeared to belong to a young man aged around 18 or 20. At first police were unsure if the skull belonged to a murder victim or if it had been discarded by grave robbers. Another theory was that it could have been put there by medical students trying to play a prank. However, on May 29 another skull was found nearby and it too appeared to belong to a young man aged between 18 and 20. Soon after, children playing in a field near Döhren found a sack that contained a number of human bones.

On June 13, a skull was found on the banks of the Leine River and another was located near a mill. Both of these skulls had been separated from the spine with a sharp instrument, and one was believed to belong to a boy in his late teens and the other to a boy aged between 11 and 13. There were marks on one of these skulls that indicated the victim had been scalped. The discovery of all these skulls had added fuel to the speculation that had been circulating for over a year regarding the disappearances of so many children and teenagers in Hanover.

A search was organized among several hundred local residents on June 8 of the areas close to the Leine River. During the search a number of human bones were discovered and given to the police. This led to the police to drag the entire portion of the river that ran through the city center. This resulted in more than 500 human bones and body parts being found, many of which had knife marks on them. A court doctor later declared the bones and remains belonged to 22 different victims, a third of which were believed to belong to young males aged between 15 and 20 years.

Haarmann quickly became a suspect because of his history of child molestation and sexual assault of a minor, and because the police were well aware he was a homosexual. Haarmann had also been connected to some of the disappearances in one way or another, including Friedel Rothe and Hermann Koch. The police decided to place Haarmann under surveillance, and because he was known to spend a lot of time at Hanover Station, two young police officers were sent to the Station to pose as undercover officers so they could watch Haarmann discreetly.

The two officers noticed Haarmann in the Station on June 22, and before long he was seen arguing with Karl Fromm, a 15-year-old boy. Haarmann approached police and demanded they arrest the boy for traveling with forged documents. After Fromm was arrested, he told police he had been with Haarmann for four days, during which time he had been raped repeatedly, often with a knife at his throat. Haarmann was arrested the next morning and charged with sexual assault of the boy.

Once Haarmann had been arrested, police were able to search his apartment and were shocked to find the walls, floors and bedding all horribly bloodstained. Haarmann tried to convince them the blood was from the meat he used to trade. On questioning his neighbors, both current and at his previous addresses, many of them commented on the large number of young teenage boys they had seen visiting Haarmann. Some neighbors even claimed they had seen Haarmann leaving his house carrying sacks and bags in the early hours of some mornings. Two tenants who had lived with him previously claimed they had followed him one morning and witnessed him throwing a sack into the Leine River in the spring of 1924.

The large number of possessions and clothing found in Haarmann's apartment was suspected to belong to the victims, and the police put them on display at the police station and invited the parents and family members of the missing boys to come and see if they could identify anything. Many of the items were identified, and Haarmann claimed he had gotten them through the black market or they had been left behind by young men who had engaged in sexual acts at his apartment.

On June 29, keys, boots and clothing found in his apartment were identified as belonging to Robert Witzel. His skull had been found in a garden back in May. His friend would go on to identify Haarmann as the man who had been pretending to be a police officer, last seen with Witzel before he disappeared. This identification flustered Haarmann and although he initially tried to talk his way out of it, the evidence and testimony was too strong. Haarmann broke down.

Haarmann's sister urged him to come clean under this mountain of evidence that had been put before them. Finally he began confessing to the rape, murder and dismemberment of multiple young men between 1918 and 1924. He referred to this period as a 'rabid sexual passion' and claimed that he never planned to kill the boys, but the urge to bite their Adam's apple would be overwhelming while in the 'throes of ecstasy'. He alleged one boy had escaped, but nobody ever came forward.

Even though Haarmann found the act of dismembering the bodies abhorrent, and he was ill for several days after his first victim, the urge to bite was far stronger than the distaste he felt at cutting the bodies into pieces. He explained to the police that the dismemberment would take place quickly after the murders, but would take up to two days to finish. Before he would start, he would make himself a very strong cup of black coffee and then would lay the body on the floor and cover the face. The first thing he would do was remove the intestines, which would be placed in a bucket.

A towel would then be used to soak up the blood gathering in the abdominal cavity, and then three cuts would be made between the ribs and the shoulders. He would then push the ribs up until the shoulders broke. The internal organs, including the heart, kidneys and lungs, would be taken out, cut up into small pieces and put in the bucket with the intestines. Then Haarmann would remove the arms and legs. He even removed the flesh from the torso and the limbs, claiming he often disposed of it in the toilet or the river.

The last part of the body Haarmann would remove was the head. Using a small knife, he would then remove all of the flesh from the bones of the skull, and then wrap the skull in rags before bashing it with an axe. This enabled Haarmann to gain access to the brain, which would also end up in the bucket. This gory bucket mixture would then be poured into the river alongside the chopped-up bones of his victims.

Despite his detailed confessions, Haarmann claimed the intact skulls found in the river did not belong to his victims, as he had smashed the skulls into pieces. The only skulls he hadn't destroyed were his first and his last victims. Haarmann stated that the murders were not premeditated, but police found evidence that contradicted this. They also began to realize during his confession that Haarmann only admitted to murders where they had shown him evidence against him. At one point he even stated there were more victims that the police didn't know about, but he wouldn't elaborate.

Haarmann claimed to have killed 50 or 70 young boys, but the police could only connect him to 27. Therefore he would only be charged with those murders. Haarmann claimed some of the murders were committed because Grans insisted, so Grans was also charged with being an accessory to murder. Before his trial, Haarmann underwent a psychological examination and was found to be fit to stand trial.

Trial and Death

The trial began on December 4, 1924, and Haarmann pleaded guilty to 14 of the 27 murders he was charged with. He claimed he was unsure if he had committed the other 13 because he wasn't sure of their identification. Grans pleaded not guilty to all charges of being an accessory to murder. The whole proceedings were conducted behind closed doors, and anyone allowed to enter the courtroom was thoroughly searched by the police beforehand. Members of the public were kept out because of the horrifying graphic details of the murders. Haarmann readily confessed to committing murder and selling the victims' possessions, but he vehemently denied ever selling the human flesh as meat. As a result of the investigation, any meat found in his apartment was tested by a doctor who confirmed none of it was human.

The trial lasted just under two weeks, even though there had been testimonies from 190 witnesses. Psychiatrists, police officers and acquaintances were amongst those called to testify, as well as the parents of the numerous victims who were called in to confirm identity of possessions found in Haarmann's apartment. The court reconvened on December 19, and Haarmann was found guilty of 24 of the 27 murders. Three of the murders he denied committing and was subsequently found not guilty. The sentence handed down to Haarmann was death by beheading, and Haarmann stood and stated he accepted the verdict. Grans, on the other hand, became hysterical when found guilty and also sentenced to death by beheading. An appeal of the sentence was never lodged by Haarmann, who believed he deserved to die for what he had done. Grans did lodge an appeal but this was rejected.

On the morning of April 15, 1925, Haarmann was led to the guillotine at Hanover Prison and beheaded at 6 am. German tradition prevents condemned men from knowing their execution date until the night before, so there is very little time to ponder what was about to take place. His final wish was to have a Brazilian coffee and an expensive cigar, which he was given while in his cell. Haarmann's last words spoken before his execution were:

"I am guilty, gentlemen, but, hard though it may be, I want to die as a man." As he placed his head on the guillotine block, he uttered: "I repent, but I do not fear death."

Timeline of Murder

Year: 1918

27 September – Friedel Rothe (17) – A runaway. Allegedly buried in Stöckener Cemetery by Haarmann.

Year: 1923

12 February – Fritz Franke (17) – Met Haarmann at the Hanover station.

20 March – Wilhelm Schulze (17) – A runaway. Clothing given to Haarmann's landlady.

23 May – Roland Huch (16) – A runaway. Last seen at Hanover station.

31 May – Hans Sonnenfeld (19) – A runaway. Clothing found in Haarmann's apartment.

25 June – Ernst Ehrenberg (13) – Neighbor's son.

24 August – Heinrich Struß (18) – Last seen at a cinema in Hanover. Haarmann had his violin case.

24 September – Paul Bronischewski (17) – Met Haarmann at

Hanover station.

30 September – Richard Gräf (17) – Told people Haarmann offered him a job.

12 October – Wilhelm Erdner (16) – Disappeared on his way to work. Haarmann sold his bicycle.

24 October – Hermann Wolf (15) – Last seen at Hanover station. Property found in Haarmann's apartment.

27 October – Heinz Brinkmann (13) – Disappeared from Hanover station. Seen with Haarmann.

10 November – Adolf Hannappel (17) – Last seen at Hanover station and seen with Haarmann.

6 December – Adolf Hennies (19) – Disappeared looking for work in Hanover. Grans had his coat.

1924

5 January – Ernst Spiecker (17) – Disappeared. Grans had his shirt.

15 January – Heinrich Koch (20) – An acquaintance of Haarmann. Clothing given to Haarmann's landlady.

2 February – Willi Senger (19) – Acquaintance of Haarmann. Haarmann had his coat.

8 February – Hermann Speichert (16) – Haarmann's landlady received his clothes and Grans had his geometry kit.

1 April – Hermann Bock (22) – Acquaintance of Haarmann and last seen going to his apartment. Haarmann was wearing Bock's suit when he was arrested.

8 April – Alfred Hogrefe (16) – A runaway. Seen often with Haarmann. Clothes in his possession.

17 April – Wilhelm Apel (16) – Lured away by Haarmann. His clothing sold by Haarmann's landlady.

26 April – Robert Witzel (18) – Disappeared. Skull was found May 20.

9 May – Heinrich Martin (14) – Disappeared from Hanover station. Possessions found in Haarmann's apartment.

26 May – Fritz Wittig (17) – Taken by Haarmann because Grans wanted his suit.

26 May – Friedrich Abeling (10) – Disappeared while playing truant. Skull found in the river June 13.

5 June – Friedrich Koch (16) Disappeared and last seen with Haarmann.

14 June – Erich de Vries (17) – Disappeared. Haarmann led police to his remains.

Crimes of Opportunity

Post-war Germany provided Fritz Haarmann with everything he needed to indulge his fantasies and to also line his pockets. It was a time when young boys were sent out alone to seek work, as families struggled with the poor economy following the war. Just about everything had a price, if you were willing to pay it, and so it was easy for Haarmann to convince these young boys that he could help them, either with work, money or food.

Haarmann was a charmer, and because he was a little feminine in his mannerisms, he most likely did not seem a threatening character, even to young boys and men. They followed him willingly back to his home, unaware that they were in any danger. Most murderers worked alone, so with Haarmann being accompanied by Grans the majority of the time, they most likely just appeared to be a couple of gentleman who were willing to help out the less fortunate young men they came across.

Hanover Station seemed to be a focal point of gathering for many young boys and men at the time. Following Haarmann's arrest, there were many who came forward who knew Haarmann and had seen him with certain missing boys, but they never thought he was capable of anything so unthinkable. That's the thing with murderers - they generally don't look bad or dangerous; instead they look like a neighbor or other member of the community.

Haarmann was clever about the victims he chose. He opted for those who were on their own, including those who were homeless or traveling for work. Therefore, they were less likely to be reported missing in a hurry. This allowed him ample time to do whatever he wanted to these poor fellows, then dispose of their bodies long before the police started looking for them. He was even brazen enough to be seen in public wearing distinctive items of clothing that had belonged to some of his victims. He thought he was infallible.

This 'Butcher of Hanover' was able to get away with his murders for a very long time, and it is unknown exactly how many he really committed. He may have admitted to 27, but it was unusual for him to suddenly start in 1918, when he was almost 40 years old.

Usually murderers start much younger, often in their early 20s. So is it possible there were more committed before then? Perhaps while he was in the military? We will never know.

If Haarmann had committed his murders in this modern era, chances are high that he would have been caught much sooner, with the advancements in forensic technology and the invention of security cameras that now grace most major transit stations around the world. But it was the environment of the time, and having ingratiated himself in the good books of the police certainly helped him, which was a very clever move on his part. Haarmann was a 'Jekyll and Hyde' - mild-mannered gentleman by day, Butcher of Hanover by night.

Media

Film:

M - (1931)

The Tenderness of the Wolves – (1973)

Der Totmacher (The Deathmaker) – (1995)

Books:

Killers: The Ruthless Exponents of Murder – Nigel Cawthorne, Geoffrey Tibballs (1993)

The Encyclopedia of Serial Killers – Brian Lane and Wilfred Gregg (1992)

Monsters of Weimar: Haarmann, the Story of a Werewolf – Theodor Lessing (1925)

The World's Most Evil Murderers: Real-Life Stories of Infamous Killers – Colin Wilson and Damon Wilson (2006)

CHAPTER 4:
Anatoly Onoprienko
– The Beast of Ukraine

One of the worst serial killers in modern history, Ukrainian Anatoly Onoprienko was a cold-blooded killer who felt no emotion or remorse for his victims. He would attack at night time, terrorizing people in their homes before violently killing them and often setting their houses on fire. Men, women and children were all just the same to Onoprienko – he just didn't care who he killed; he just needed to satisfy his bloodlust. With a death toll of 52, Onoprienko was nicknamed the Beast of Ukraine, The Terminator and Citizen O, and was a real-life monster.

An Abandoned Child

Onoprienko was born in July 1959 in a village called Lasky. He had an older brother 13 years his senior, and his father Yuri had received medals for bravery during his service in World War I. At 4 years of age, Onoprienko's mother passed away, and he was left in the care of his aunt and grandparents for a while before being given to an orphanage. His brother, Valentin, continued to live with their father, and Onoprienko always resented his father for giving him away but keeping his brother. He would later say that he believed this is what determined his destiny.

Chilling Tales of Murder

Onoprienko would enter a house at night and kill everyone inside, and his murders always followed a specific pattern. He would always look for a house that was isolated, and then create a commotion to get the attention of the people inside. The first person in the house he would kill was always the adult male, and then he would seek out the wife and kill her before killing any children in the home. Usually he would then set the house on fire to hide any evidence. If anyone happened to witness this or cross his path while he was on a rampage, they would also be eliminated.

When he was first arrested, he only admitted to killing eight victims, but before long he finally confessed to taking the lives of 52 people. During his police interviews, he would recount each murder in detail, with no signs of emotion. He claimed he hadn't always worked alone, and his first murders were committed with his accomplice Serhiy Rogozin. In 1989, they had robbed 9 people and then killed them.

Onoprienko claimed he didn't get any pleasure from committing murder, he just felt an urge to do so. He referred to dead bodies as being 'ugly' and said they smell bad and sent out 'bad vibes'.

Apparently he once sat in his car with the bodies of five people he had killed while he tried to decide what to do with them, and the smell was unbearable. Although he had an accomplice to start with, apart from the initial nine victims, the rest were committed by Onoprienko alone.

According to Onoprienko, one night he killed the parents of a young girl, and while she huddled on top of her bed praying, he ordered her to show him where her parents kept their money. She apparently looked at him defiantly and refused. He said her strength was incredible, but he still felt nothing as he smashed in her head. He would often shoot the adults and bash the children with heavy objects. And he always robbed the homes of any valuables so he could sell them.

Following are the murders Onoprienko confessed to and the details as he recalled them.

Victims 1-10

In 1989 Onoprienko and Rogozin were interrupted by a family of ten while they were robbing the house. There were two adults and eight children, and they slaughtered them all. After this event, Onoprienko never had contact with Rogozin again.

Victims 11-15

Onoprienko came across five people sleeping in a car he was planning to burglarize. One of the victims was an 11-year old-boy, and all were shot dead before the car was set on fire.

Victims 16-19

On Christmas Eve 1995, Onoprienko entered the home of the Zaichenko family intending to rob it. He carried with him a sawn-off double-barreled shotgun, and killed the family of four before setting fire to the house.

Victims 20-24

On the night of January 2, 1996, Onoprienko killed a family of four. As he was leaving, he came across a man walking down the road and shot him also to remove a potential witness.

Victims 25-28

Onoprienko claimed to have killed four people on the night of January 6, 1996, but this time they weren't together or inside a house. Instead he would stop cars on the highway, then shoot and kill the drivers. Victims included a Navy ensign called Kasai; Savitsky, a taxi driver; Kochergina, a cook; and another unidentified victim.

Victims 29-35

The Pilat family of five was killed on January 17, 1996. As usual their house was then set on fire. Onoprienko then killed two possible witnesses, a pedestrian called Zakharko, 56, and a railroad worker called Kondzela, 27.

Victims 36-39

A woman, Marusina, her two sons and a visitor were all shot and killed on January 30, 1996.

Victims 40-43

Onoprienko entered the Dubchak family home on the night of February 19, 1996, and shot the father and son dead. He then killed the mother and the daughter with a hammer.

Victims 44-48

The Bodnarchuk family was murdered at home on February 27, 1996. Onoprienko shot the two adults in the house to death, then attacked the two little girls, aged 7 and 8, with an axe. He was still in the house an hour later when he noticed a neighbor walking around outside. He proceeded to shoot and kill the man, and then hacked at his body with the axe.

Victims 49-52

The last known victims of Onoprienko were the Novosad family. On March 22, 1996, he shot and killed all four members of the family then set the house alight.

Catching the Beast

A nationwide manhunt was launched in March 1996, which included the services of 2,000 police officers and 3,000 military troops. They concentrated mainly on the areas where the murders had taken place. During the hunt, the police arrested Yury Mozola, a 26-year-old man, and detained him for questioning about the murders. For three days he was beaten, burned and subjected to electric shocks, as the police tried to force him to confess. Mozola refused to confess, claiming his innocence, and at the end of three days of torture, he died from the treatment he was given. Subsequently, those that had been involved in beating and torturing Mozola were prosecuted and sent to prison, albeit for short terms.

Meanwhile, Onoprienko had asked his cousin, Pyotr Onoprienko if he could move in with him for a while, and Pyotr agreed. However, he was concerned when he discovered the stash of weapons Onoprienko had brought into the house. He confronted Onoprienko, at which point Onoprienko became threatening, and he was asked to leave the house. Onoprienko ended up moving in with his girlfriend and her children.

Pyotr still felt deeply concerned about the threats Onoprienko had made towards his family, so he notified the police on April 16 about the stash of weapons he had seen with Onoprienko. When he mentioned to the deputy police chief that one of the weapons was a 12-gauge rifle, the same weapon used in one of the local murders, their interest increased. The police superiors at police headquarters were notified and the deputy police chief was instructed to create a task force and search Onoprienko's home address.

An hour later, more than twenty detectives and patrolmen had been gathered and headed for Onoprienko's apartment he shared with his girlfriend, all in unmarked cars. All exits for the building were blocked off, and the other floors of the building were guarded by officers. They ensured they had the building surrounded before approaching the apartment. Police were unsure if Onoprienko's girlfriend and her children were at home, but as it turned out, they were actually at church but expected home at any time. Therefore, when the officers rang the doorbell, Onoprienko automatically opened the door thinking it was them returning home. This made it much easier for the police to subdue and handcuff Onoprienko.

Onoprienko was asked for his identification, and the officers followed him to a closet. As the door was opened for him, Onoprienko immediately went to grab a pistol he had hidden inside the closet, but he was overcome quickly and unable to reach it. Ironically, that same pistol had been stolen at one of the murder scenes. Onoprienko was taken to the station while officers continued to search the apartment. They would find 122 items that had been listed as being stolen from a number of murder scenes. During the search, Onoprienko's girlfriend returned home, and when she was told what he had done, she was genuinely shocked. She had been led to believe he was some type of businessman and she had believed him.

It didn't take long for Onoprienko to confess to his crimes. Luckily for him, the death penalty was in the process of being abolished, so there was a good chance he may receive a life sentence. He still had to go to trial though, and he had plenty of time to prepare, thanks to a rather bizarre Ukrainian law. A trial cannot start until the defendant has had the chance to read every piece of evidence against him, and he can take as long as he needs to do so. In this case, there were 99 volumes of information, including photos of the victims, the burnt-down houses and burnt cars, and the items stolen from each murder scene.

Authorities were deeply concerned about the period of time when Onoprienko was overseas. Between 1989 and 1995, he had left the Ukraine and traveled through Europe. Nobody really knows what he did during that period, or even where he was. What is known is that he was deported by both the German and Austrian embassies, but they declined to give details as to why or when. Therefore, it is possible that Onoprienko had committed even more murders than what was accounted for. However, because Onoprienko wanted to have a higher body count than Chikatilo, you would think that if there were more victims, he would willingly confess to those as well.

The trial was further delayed due to lack of funding. Under the law, the court is required to pay for the hotel and travel bills for each witness, and with 400 witnesses being called, the expenditure wasn't a priority in the economically strapped Ukraine. Eventually the judge was forced to make a televised appeal aimed at the government to provide the funding. Finally, the trial started on November 24, 1998.

Following a psychiatric assessment, the court ruled on February 12, 1999, that Onoprienko was fit to stand trial, despite his claims that he had been hearing voices since his childhood. No psychiatric disease could be found, and Onoprienko was deemed to understand what he had done and was in control of his actions at the time of the murders.

The next upheaval came when Onoprienko demanded a new state-appointed attorney. He requested a lawyer that was a minimum of 50 years old, half or full Jewish, with international experience and economic independence. This request was refused, and Onoprienko refused to testify any further. Because he was now being uncooperative, Onoprienko was put into a metal cage and remained there throughout the court proceedings.

His attitude and arrogance deteriorated further. When asked if he wanted to make a statement at the beginning of the trial, Onoprienko shrugged his shoulders and said no. When informed of his right to object to the proceedings, he stated it was their law and he was a hostage. Onoprienko stated he had no nationality, but when the judge replied that it wasn't possible, Onoprienko rolled his eyes and stated that, according to the law enforcement officers, he was Ukrainian.

The people who had come to witness the court hearing were getting angry at the attitude Onoprienko was displaying, and the judge had to call the court to order on many occasions. Abuse was being shouted at Onoprienko, and calls were made for him to die a slow, agonizing death. Others claimed the beast should be tortured, or cut into shreds. Some of those who had come to watch had traveled hundreds of miles, and it seemed Onoprienko was making a mockery of the whole thing.

During the trial, President Kuchma declared Onoprienko should receive the death penalty because his crimes were so heinous. He felt the Council of Europe should grant the execution because of the exceptionally cruel and sadistic nature of the case. The human rights group, Amnesty International, criticized the President, saying his statements could have affected the outcome of Onoprienko's trial.

All of the prosecution's witnesses failed to turn up to court. When the first murder was being discussed, the judge read out a telegram from the witnesses who claimed they were unable to attend due to family circumstances. However, the testimony of witnesses wasn't really necessary, as nobody had actually seen him commit the crimes. Those that had were already dead. When Rogozin was questioned, he denied having any part of the murders, and said Onoprienko was an intelligent and kind man.

Despite the government trying to abolish the death penalty, Onoprienko was convicted of the murders and sentenced to death by shooting. Rogozin was sent to prison for 13 years.

The Shocking Confessions of a Madman

"To me it was like hunting. Hunting people down."

Onoprienko stated that he would be bored and have nothing to do when he would suddenly get the idea to kill. He claimed he would do anything he could think of to try and stop himself thinking that way, but he was unable to. So, he would go out and murder innocent people.

During his interviews, Onoprienko claimed to have had a vision from God who commanded him to commit murder, and nine days later, he killed a family and burned down their house. Following his arrest, Onoprienko was interviewed over the next five days by a doctor, Teslya, who later referred to Onoprienko as the 'most perplexing man I've ever interviewed'. Onoprienko claimed he was chosen by God and that he was superior, and believed he had very strong hypnotic powers. He said he could telepathically control animals and had the ability to stop his own heart using his mind. When asked to use his hypnotic powers on the doctor, however, Onoprienko said it wouldn't work, as it only worked on weak people.

At one point during these interviews, Onoprienko claimed he had been diagnosed previously with schizophrenia and had spent time in a hospital in Kiev. Teslya was not able to investigate this by law. However, shortly after his arrest, a statement was made by the Kiev Interior Ministry that Onoprienko was an outpatient, and his therapists had known he was a murderer. No further information regarding his diagnosis or admissions to hospital were released from Kiev.

After his week of interviews, Teslya came to the conclusion that Onoprienko was, in fact, insane and that he had acted on his own despite rumors of a gang being involved. Despite Teslya's impressions, the Ukrainian court determined Onoprienko was, in fact, mentally competent and fit to stand trial. Onoprienko himself didn't believe he was insane or a crazy person – he believed he had special powers and was ordered to kill. He referred to a time when he wanted to kill his brother's wife because he despised her, but he couldn't because he hadn't been 'ordered' to.

'Kill me or I will kill again'

Onoprienko had never shown any remorse for his actions, and while incarcerated, he had made a statement to the press that he wanted to be the world record holder for committing murders. In his own words, he said "If I am ever let out, I will start killing again, but this time it will be worse, ten times worse". He said the urge to kill was always present, and he believed he was being 'groomed' to serve the devil, Satan. Onoprienko also stated that if he were to escape, he would hunt down the president and 'hang him from a tree by his testicles'.

Throughout his trial, Onoprienko kept quiet, only speaking when he absolutely had to. But once incarcerated, he freely made comments and spoke to the media. He stated to one newspaper that he preferred receiving the death sentence as he had no interest in having relationships with people. He also stated he was shocked at how people had seemed indifferent to his acts of murder. During one murderous rampage, the victims had been screaming so loudly they could have been heard throughout the village, yet nobody came to their assistance.

Onoprienko gave a slight insight into his emotional mindset when he talked about the first animal he had killed. He said he had shot a deer, and he felt really upset when he saw the dead animal. He was upset more because there was no reason for him to kill the deer, and he felt sorry for the animal. But he claimed he never felt that way ever again. He never felt sorry for the people he killed, seeing them more as masses rather than individual human beings.

On August 27, 2013, Onoprienko suffered heart failure while incarcerated and died. He was 54 years old.

Timeline of Horror

December 12 1995

A forestry teacher with the surname of Zaichenko was killed along with his wife and his two small children, one of who was only 3 months old. Murders took place in Gamarnya, Zhitomirskaya Oblast.

December 31 1995

A man by the name of Kryuchkov, his wife and his two sisters were murdered and the house set alight. A potential witness called Malinsky was killed out on the street. Location was Bratkovichi.

January 5 1996

Two men called Dolinin and Odintsov were shot while sitting in their broken down car in Energodar, Zaporozhskaya Oblast. Later, a pedestrian called Garmash and a patrolman named Pybalko were killed in Vasilyvevka-Dneiprorudny.

January 6 1996

Navy ensign Kasai, a kolkhoz cook named Kochergina and a taxi driver named Savitsky were killed when their cars were stopped on the highway near Berdyansk-Dnieprovskaya.

January 17 1996

Five members of the Pilat family were shot and killed and their house set on fire. Two witnesses were killed later, a female railroad worker named Kondzela and a train passenger named Zakharko. The location was Bratkovichi.

January 30 1996

A driver, Zagranichniy and a nurse named Marusina were killed along with her two sons, in Fastove, Kievskaya Oblast.

February 19 1996

Four members of the Dubchak are family were killed. The father and his son were shot while the mother and daughter were mauled with a hammer. The location was Olevsk, Zhitomirskaya Oblast.

February 27 1996

The Bodnarchuk family of four was killed. The adults were shot to death and the young children were hacked with an axe. A businessman named Tsalk was killed by gunshot and being hacked to death with the axe. Location was Malina, Lvivskaya Oblast.

March 22 1996

Four members of the Novosad family were shot and killed in Bratkovichi and their house set on fire.

The Families Left Behind

When a loved one is brutally murdered, it can have a terrible effect on the family members left behind. But when you lose an entire family unit, such as the case with these murders, the remaining family is completely destroyed. It is difficult enough to mourn and grieve for one victim, let alone four or five. Whole lives can be ruined because of the actions of a killer.

Anatoly Grishenko lost his wife Galina to Onoprienko in the first murders. As hard as it was to lose his beloved wife and mother of his teenage son, the months and years it took for the trial to even take place was soul destroying. The toll it took on Anatoly left him a broken man. For him, it was easy for Onoprienko to sit in his cell reading his case notes for as long as he wanted while Anatoly waited for justice to be done.

Like when anything comes to an end, you seek closure so you can move forward. When a loved one dies, you never forget, but you can learn to carry on if the case is closed and the right justice has been served on the perpetrator. It is difficult enough as it is to listen to all the testimony and gruesome details during a trial, making you relive the whole experience over and over. But when you are waiting for such a long time for the trial to start, the murder stays on your mind every minute of the day. Onoprienko may have physically killed Galina, but he was also slowly killing Anatoly.

While Anatoly was being interviewed about how his wife's murder had affected him, his teenage boy hid in the kitchen where it was dark. Since his mother had been taken from him, he no longer liked to meet people. This boy's life was forever changed because of Onoprienko.

Understanding the Beast

Anatoly Onoprienko was the epitome of nightmares. He would seek out homes that were relatively isolated, and under the cover of darkness would break his way in, then brutally murder every person in the house. He was a man so cold that he could have a conversation with a young child moments before bashing her to death with a hammer. Onoprienko was the man you would lie in bed at night and pray he didn't knock on your door.

Onoprienko initially was a burglar, breaking into homes and stealing whatever he could get his hands on so he could sell it on and make some money. The first murders he committed were during such a burglary, and he killed the family in the house so there would be no witnesses. These murders were more a case of killing out of perceived necessity. But, from then on, his objective seemed to change. Sure, he still robbed the houses he entered, but financial gain was no longer the reason behind his actions.

After the first murders, Onoprienko developed a taste for killing, and he began entering homes at night for the purpose of killing the occupants. He would always shoot the adults first, to remove potential threats, and then he would target the children. But when he killed the children, he chose to either attack them with a hammer or sometimes an axe. These murders were up close and brutal, unlike the somewhat 'clean' shooting deaths of the adults. It's almost as though the children were the real targets and the adults just got in the way.

Onoprienko said himself that he would never stop killing, and that the only way to stop him was to execute him. He claimed when first interviewed that he tried to stop himself when the urges came, but he obviously didn't try hard enough. He could easily have gone to a medical professional, a psychiatrist or even the authorities and sought help for these thoughts he was having. But he chose not to. The truth of the matter is that he simply enjoyed the act of taking another person's life.

In his own explanation, Onoprienko claimed he had no feelings of remorse, sympathy or empathy for his victims. He just didn't care about what he had done or how it affected the loved ones left behind to grieve. The only important thing to him was how it made him feel. Like a blood lust, Onoprienko went out night after night seeking more victims. He tried to make sure he wasn't caught either, by eliminating any potential witnesses. But then he started to kill more randomly, such as the victims driving down the road.

He was out of control.

There are records in existence that show Onoprienko had schizophrenia, but these have never been released. Some of his behaviors, statements and beliefs certainly seem to back up this diagnosis. But this doesn't make a man a cold-blooded killer. Onoprienko wanted to hold the world record for murder victims. He went to his death knowing that he had failed in that quest.

CHAPTER 5:

Cho Seung-Hui – Virginia Tech Massacre

On April 16, 2007, a lone man walked into the buildings at Virginia Polytechnic Institute and State University in Virginia and opened fire on the students and teachers who were going about their usual days. The man responsible was Cho Seung-Hui, also pronounced Seung-Hui Cho, a fellow undergraduate student, and he continued to fire upon anyone he came across until the massacre was ended with his own death.

A Mentally Ill Child

In the South Korean city of Asan, Cho was born on January 18, 1984. His family ended up spending a couple of years living in Seoul before they immigrated to America. Although his father had his own business in Seoul, the money he made was not enough to fully support his family, so seeking a better life for them all, he made the decision to take his wife and three children to the US. At the time, Cho was 8 years old. Initially the family settled in Detroit before deciding to move to Washington, because there was a large South Korean community there. Cho's parents bought a dry-cleaning business and eventually the family became permanent residents of America.

As a child, some of the extended family who stayed in South Korea felt there was a problem with Cho's behavior. They believed he had a mental illness, as he did not mix with other children and he never said much. His own great-aunt thought Cho was cold and shy, though he was well-behaved. Cho's grandfather also sensed there was a problem because the child never tried to hug him, would not make eye contact and wouldn't call him grandfather.

Cho's School Days

Cho was a good student academically, and while at Elementary School, he was able to complete a three-year program in just one-and-a-half years. He was particularly good at English and mathematics, and he was often used as an example for the other pupils. Children didn't dislike him, so he wasn't completely antisocial. One school acquaintance later spoke of how Cho would cry every day after school saying he didn't want to go back, but there didn't seem to be a reason for his hatred of going to school.

When Cho was in the eighth grade, in 1999, the shocking Columbine High School massacre occurred, and the newspapers and media were flooded with articles and reports on the tragic incident. A fellow student commented that Cho seemed to be obsessed or transfixed by the tragedy, and had even written on his book binder 'f' you all, I hope you all burn in hell'. At this time, Cho also submitted a school assignment he had written saying he wanted to repeat what had happened at Columbine. The school immediately contacted Cho's older sister, who informed their parents, and an appointment was made for Cho to see a psychiatrist.

Following his appointments with the psychiatrist, Cho was diagnosed with a social anxiety disorder called selective mutism, meaning he was unwilling to speak. This resulted in him having strange speech patterns, and he was bullied throughout high school for it. Apparently when Cho was called, he would look down and not speak or make eye contact. At one point, one of his teachers had threatened to fail Cho for failing to participate in the classroom, so Cho started reading out loud, but his voice was strange, sounding as though he had something in his mouth. Although Cho was bullied from time to time, most of the students just left him alone.

While still in high school, treatments and therapies were put into place to deal with Cho's selective mutism. He was put into a special education unit because he classified under 'emotional disturbance' and he was excused from having to speak in front of the class. He was given less than an hour of speech therapy per month, and he received mental health therapy until he refused the treatment after his junior year.

Putting their faith in God, Cho's parents thought that if they took him to church, he may be cured of his afflictions. Cho did not have the same religious beliefs as his parents, and a former pastor at their church later commented that he never heard Cho even speak one sentence. The pastor had suggested to Cho's mother that he may be autistic and urged her to take him to the hospital for assessment, but she refused.

When Cho enrolled at Virginia Tech, none of his medical or mental health records could be given to the admissions staff as per the federal law that forbids disclosure without the person's consent. Therefore the Tech was unaware Cho had selective mutism and other anxiety problems. He became an undergraduate major in business information technology, but by the time he reached his senior year, he had switched his major to English. Cho lived on campus, in a dormitory called Harper Hall, with five roommates.

A major issue occurred in fall 2005, when Cho's poetry teacher, Professor Nikki Giovanni, had him removed from the class. The Professor found Cho had a menacing mean streak, and she found his writing very intimidating. He had also taken photos of female student's legs from under the desks and wrote obscene poetry tinged with violence. The professor was so concerned about Cho that she was prepared to resign rather than continue to teach him, and after writing a letter to Lucinda Roy, the department head, Cho was removed from the poetry class. Because of the nature of the complaint, Roy notified the dean's office, student affairs office and the campus police about Cho, but each department stated they could do nothing unless there were specific and overt threats made.

Roy had actually been Cho's teacher the previous year in her poetry class, and she too had serious concerns about his behavior. Although Cho was intelligent, he also appeared to be insecure, awkward and lonely, and he would wear sunglasses in class. Roy described Cho as being obnoxious and arrogant sometimes, and she found his writing to have an angry tone. He would often take photos of his teacher in the classroom, and on the rare occasions he spoke, he would whisper. Wanting to help him, Roy agreed to tutor Cho outside of the classroom, but before long she began to feel unsafe with him. Roy felt so concerned that she had given her assistant a 'code' name she would use if she needed security, and she strongly urged Cho to undertake some counseling.

Witnesses claimed that during Cho's senior year, he never seemed to be studying or going to classes. Instead he would sit in his room typing on his laptop, or would go to the dining hall for food. He was also seen riding a bicycle round in circles in the parking lot at one point. Cho preferred to sit in a chair by the window and look at the lawn down below for long periods of time.

Two students who had shared a room with Cho between 2005 and 2006 noticed some bizarre behavior changes in Cho. John Eide and Andy Koch had noticed Cho seemed to exhibit repetitive and obsessive behaviors, and would listen to a particular song repeatedly. He also wrote the lyrics from that song on the wall of the dormitory room. Ironically, those lyrics were 'teach me how to speak/teach me how to share/teach me where to go' from the song 'Shine', by Collective Soul. One night, Koch discovered Cho in the doorway taking pictures of him, and he would also make multiple harassing type phone calls to Koch referring to himself as 'Question Mark' or 'Cho's brother'. The two young men were so concerned by Cho's behavior that once while Cho was out of the room, they searched it but only found a pocket knife.

During Thanksgiving, when many students go home for the holiday, Cho placed a call to Koch and told him he was on holiday with Vladimir Putin. Although both Koch and Eide had initially tried to be friends with Cho, they slowly stopped talking to him and told their female friends to never visit their room. Cho had embarked on stalking female students, and Koch and Eide recalled at least three of these incidents. Two resulted in Cho being given verbal warnings by the campus police. The first incident took place on November 27, 2005, when Cho sent an instant message to a female student and managed to find out where she was staying on the campus. He then visited her room, and Cho told Eide that he had introduced himself as Question Mark, and the girl had been freaked out by it. The girl reported the incident and Cho was told by campus police to stay away from her.

Another incident occurred on December 13, 2005, and Cho had once again been contacting a female student via instant messaging. The student was actually a friend of Koch's. Cho found out where she lived and left a Shakespeare quote from Romeo and Juliet on the board on her door. She wasn't terribly concerned until Koch messaged her and warned her that Cho had already been in trouble for stalking other female students. Koch thought Cho was schizophrenic and urged his friend to report Cho to campus police, which she did. Cho was issued another warning to avoid contact.

Later that day, Koch received a message from Cho stating that he may as well kill himself. Thinking Cho had become suicidal, Koch called his father and asked him for advice on what to do. Koch and his father then contacted the campus authorities, and the campus police came to the room and escorted Cho to the mental health agency in Virginia. He was subsequently deemed to be mentally unwell and needing hospitalization. His mood was described as depressed with a flat affect, but Cho denied he was having suicidal thoughts. Still, he was considered to be a danger to himself and others and was detained while waiting for a commitment hearing.

The district court agreed that he was a danger to himself and others, but recommended Cho receive his treatment as an outpatient instead of an inpatient. He was released straight away, and because he had only had a basic assessment, a firm diagnosis was never made. Tragically, if Cho had been involuntarily committed to the mental health facility, he would never have been legally able to purchase firearms.

Cho's parents never gave up on trying to find help for their son, though perhaps they were looking in the wrong areas. They had repeatedly sought strength and assistance from a variety of churches, to no avail. As his behavior continued to deteriorate, his mother became increasingly concerned, but once Cho turned 18, there was nothing his parents could do anymore to help him. They had lost their influence they once had over him and had no legal rights or authority over him. The only person that could help him now, was himself.

Deadly Attack at Virginia Tech

On the morning of April 16, 2007, Cho armed himself with a 9mm semi-automatic Glock 19 handgun and a .22-caliber Walther P22 semi-automatic handgun and carried with him extra ammunition. He was about to do the unthinkable.

West Ambler Johnston

The West Ambler Johnston Hall was a co-ed residence that was home to 895 students. The doors were unlocked at 10 am, so if you wanted to enter you would need to use a magnetic key to prevent strangers or others from entering without permission. However, because Cho's mailbox was located in the lobby, he had a card that enabled him to enter after 7:30 am. But this didn't explain how he was able to enter earlier, as his first attack occurred at approximately 7:15 am.

Cho made his way to the room that was shared by Emily J. Hilscher, a freshman, and another student who wasn't there at the time. He entered and shot 19-year-old Emily. Ryan C. Clark, a 22-year-old male resident assistant, heard the gunshots and rushed to help Hilscher. Cho then shot Clark and killed him. Hilscher didn't die immediately, and managed to stay alive for three hours before breathing her last breath.

Leaving the scene, Cho then went back to his Harper Hall room, which was just to the west of West Ambler. By now the emergency services had been called and responded to West Ambler, not knowing that Cho was in the building next door changing out of his clothes that were now bloodstained. Once redressed, Cho logged on to his laptop and deleted his email and took out the hard drive. An hour after he had shot the two students in West Ambler, a witness saw him near the duck pond on campus, and it was suspected he had thrown his hard drive and his phone in there. Despite searching by the police, these items were never located.

It was now nearly two hours after he had killed his first victims, and Cho had gone to the post office, mailing a package to NBC News, which contained videos and writings by Cho. The postmark on the parcel read 9:01 am. Cho then made his way to Norris Hall, and his backpack was now filled with a variety of weapons including the guns, a knife, a hammer, up to fifteen magazines and almost 400 rounds of ammunition. He was ready to embark on the second attack he had planned.

Norris Hall

Norris Hall was home to the Engineering Science and Mechanics program and others, and when Cho entered the building, he used chains to hold the three entrance doors shut. On one of the doors he attached a note claiming that if anyone tried to open the door, a bomb would go off. A faculty member actually found the note and took it to notify the administration department of the school. At that same time, Cho had started to shoot at the teachers and students on the floor below, and the emergency services were never notified of the alleged bomb threat.

Before he started shooting, Cho was seen looking into the classrooms, and students assumed he was a lost student, even though that seemed a bit strange given they were already into the semester. Cho opened fire at around 9:40 am in the advanced hydrology engineering class. Professor G.V. Loganathan was shot and killed first, and he then fired upon the thirteen students in the room. He killed nine of them and injured another two. He then crossed the hall and entered room 207, a German class, and killed the teacher, Jamie Bishop, and four of the students. Another six students were wounded in this room. The next two classrooms he entered were rooms 211 and 204.

By now the teachers and students in those rooms had heard the gunshots coming from the other rooms and they attempted to barricade the doors to prevent the gunman from entering. Professor Liviu Librescu tried to hold the door of room 204 closed, and managed to hold Cho back while many of the students escaped through the windows. Professor Librescu had been an Israeli Holocaust survivor, yet he was to fall victim to Cho, having been shot multiple times right through the closed door. However, his bravery had resulted in only one of his students being killed.

In room 211, student Henry Lee and instructor Jocelyne Couture-Nowak had attempted to barricade the door, but they failed. Both were shot and killed. A total of eleven students were shot and killed in room 211, and the other six students were wounded. One of the students, Clay Violand, later stated that he had survived by playing dead, and managed to avoid being wounded at all.

Cho went back to some of the classrooms after he had reloaded his weapons. In room 207, when he had initially left, the students had managed to barricade the door and were trying to take care of those who were wounded. When Cho came back, both Derek O'Dell and Katelyn Carney were injured as they held the door closed. In room 206, Cho had been looking at a student when Waleed Shaalan, wounded earlier, moved, which got Cho's attention. He then shot Shaalan again, this time killing him. The professor and students in room 205 had successfully barricaded their door, and Cho was unable to enter the room at all. He did fire through the door several times, but failed to hit anyone. At the end of the incident, nobody from that room was killed or injured.

Another hero of the day was Professor Kevin Granata, whose office was on the third floor. He heard the commotion coming from the rooms beneath him and he quickly ushered twenty students into his office so they could lock themselves in. Granata then made his way down the stairs to see what was going on and was shot and killed. All of the students he had taken to his office survived.

In room 211, the massacre was about to come to an end. The second attack had lasted for about twelve minutes, when Cho raised his Glock 19 to his temple and shot himself. He had killed 32 people and wounded a further seventeen. Each victim had been shot a minimum of three times, and twenty-eight of those killed had received head shots. He had fired approximately 174 rounds, and there were a further 203 live rounds found in Norris Hall during the investigation.

The Ones Who Were Killed

Jocelyne Couture-Nowak - (49) French professor – Montreal, Quebec

Jamie Bishop – (35) – German instructor – Pine Mountain, Georgia

Kevin Granata – (45) – Professor of Engineering – Toledo, Ohio

G.V. Loganathan – (53) – Professor of Engineering – Gobichettipalayam, India

Liviu Librescu – (76) – Professor of Engineering – Ploiesti, Romania

Ross Alameddine – (20) – sophomore English/Business – Saugus, Massachusetts

Ryan Clark – (22) – senior in Biology/Psych/English – Martinez, Georgia

Brian Bluhm – (25) – Master's student Civil Engineering – Louisville, Kentucky

Austin Cloyd – (18) – freshman French/International Studies – Champaign, Illinois

Caitlin Hammaren – (19) – sophomore French/International

Studies – Westtown, New York

Daniel Perez Cueva – (21) – junior International Studies – Woodbridge, Virginia

Jeremy Herbstritt – (27) – Master's student Civil Engineering – Bellefonte, Pennsylvania

Matthew Gwaltney – (24) – Master's student Environmental Engineering – Chesterfield, Virginia

Rachael Hill – (18) – freshman Biological Sciences – Richmond, Virginia

Matthew La Porte – (20) – sophomore Political Science – Dumont, New Jersey

Emily Hilscher – (19) – freshman Animal Sciences – Woodville, Virginia

Henry Lee – (20) – freshman Computer Engineering – Roanoke, Virginia/Vietnam

Jarrett Lane – (22) – senior Civil Engineering – Narrows, Virginia

Lauren McCain – (20) – freshman International Studies – Hampton, Virginia

Partahi Lumbantoruan – (34) PhD student Civil Engineering – Medan, Indonesia

Daniel O'Neil – (22) – Master's student Environmental Engineering – Lincoln, Rhode Island

Minal Panchal – (26) – Master's student Architecture – Mumbai, India

Juan Ortiz – (26) – Master's student Civil Engineering – Bayamon, Puerto Rico

Michael Pohle Jr. – (23) – senior Biological Sciences – Flemington, New Jersey

Erin Peterson – (18) – freshman International Studies – Centreville, Virginia

Julia Pryde – (23) – Master's student Biological Systems Engineering – Middletown, New Jersey

Mary Karen Read – (19) – freshman Interdisciplinary Studies – Annandale, Virginia

Waleed Shaalan – (32) – PhD student Civil Engineering – Zagazig, Egypt

Reema Samaha – (18) – freshman Urban Planning – Centreville, Virginia

Maxine Turner – (22) – senior Chemical Engineering – Vienna, Virginia

Leslie Sherman – (20) – junior International Studies/History – Springfield, Virginia

Nicolas White – (20) – junior International Studies – Smithfield, Virginia

Preparations and Plans

Cho had planned and prepared well in advance of the date of the massacre. Knowing there was a 30- day stand down period when purchasing guns, he purchased his first weapon on February 9, 2007. The second gun was purchased on March 13 from a licensed dealer in Roanoke. There are strict rules about gun purchases, and he was able to pass the background checks by presenting his

Virginia driver's permit, his US permanent residence card and his checkbook which showed his address was in Virginia. He failed to disclose he had been court ordered to attend mental health outpatient treatments, and if he had done so, his gun purchases would not have gone ahead.

Cho bought two 10-round magazines for the Walther P22 pistol through eBay on March 22, and later examination of his computer suggested he bought another one on March 23. He had also purchased jacketed hollow-point bullets. This ammunition causes a lot more damage to the tissues of the body because they expand when they enter the body. When Cho sent his manifesto to NBC, he also included a photo of the bullets which was captioned 'all the [shit] you've given me, right back at you with hollow points'.

Motive and Manifesto

After the massacre, the police found a note while searching Cho's room which contained criticisms of rich kids, deceitful charlatans and debauchery. The note also contained the statement 'you caused me to do this'. In one of his many video recordings, Cho had mentioned martyrs Eric and Dylan, and it is almost certain he is talking about Eric Harris and Dylan Klebold, the Columbine High School shooters.

The package Cho had posted on the morning of the massacre contained a DVD which held photographs and video clips as well as a manifesto which supposedly explained why Cho had attacked and killed his fellow students and faculty members. The return address on the package was from an 'A. Ishmael' and was meant to be delivered on April 17, but it had the wrong street address and zip code, so was delayed. During his autopsy, it was noted Cho had the words 'Ismail Ax' written on his arm in red ink.

The package arrived at NBC on April 18, and they immediately contacted the police to notify them. However, they also decided to publicize some of what the package contained, which turned out to be a controversial decision. Some claimed that by showing Cho's photos and videos he was being glorified in a sense and this could result in copycat murders. Those who had lost loved ones at the hands of Cho were also distressed and upset by the publishing of Cho's manifesto and asked for it to stop airing.

Despite the amount of material in Cho's manifesto and videos, the police found there was little contained in it that would explain why Cho went on his deadly rampage. A doctor who was asked to review the material claimed Cho's rantings gave minimal insight into his mental health. Instead of helping them to understand him, they came across as a PR tape, nothing like the man he usually was, meek and quiet.

Included on the DVD were 43 photographs, 25 minutes of video recordings, 23 PDF files and 23 pages of writing. His manifesto had references to the Columbine killers, and there were many references to Christianity and hedonism. He also expressed a lot of anger about wrongs that had been done to him, but he did not elaborate what those were. This was the transcript of one of his videos:

"I didn't have to do this. I could have left. I could have fled. But no, I will no longer run. If not for me, for my children, for my brothers and sisters that you fucked; I did it for them...When the time came, I did it. I had to...You had a hundred billion chances and ways to have avoided today, but you decided to spill my blood. You forced me into a corner and gave me only one option. The decision was yours. Now you have blood on your hands that will never wash off.

You sadistic snobs. I may be nothing but a piece of dogshit. You have vandalized my heart, raped my soul, and torched my conscience. You thought it was one pathetic boy's life you were extinguishing. Thanks to you, I die like Jesus Christ, to inspire generations of the weak and defenseless people.

Do you know what it feels to be spit on your face and have trash shoved down your throat? Do you know what it feels like to dig your own grave? Do you know what it feels like to have your throat slashed from ear to ear: Do you know what it feels like to be torched alive? Do you know what it feels like to be humiliated and be impaled upon a cross? And left to bleed to death for your amusement? You have never felt a single ounce of pain your whole life. Did you want to inject as much misery in our lives as you can just because you can? You had everything you wanted. Your Mercedes wasn't enough, you brats. Your golden necklaces weren't enough, you snobs. Your trust fund wasn't enough. Your vodka and cognac weren't enough. All your debaucheries weren't enough. Those weren't enough to fulfill your hedonistic needs. You had everything.

(unclear) crucified me. You loved inducing cancer in my head, terrorizing my heart, and raping my soul all this time.

When the time came, I did it...I had to."

The Aftermath

In the days immediately following the massacre, people had constructed numerous memorials for those who were killed and injured, and placed them in a variety of places on campus. Flowers were left by students, families and the general public, at the base of the observation podium located in front of Burruss Hall.

At a later time, the Hokies United, who were made up of an alliance of the different student organizations on campus that was created to respond in times of tragedy, laid 32 pieces of Hokie Stone, each bearing the name of a victim, as a temporary memorial at the foot of the observation podium. These were later replaced by a formal memorial comprised of 32 blocks of Hokie Stone standing upright with the victims' names engraved on each one. These stones were set in a semicircle at the bottom of the podium, and the families of the victims were offered the original stones.

On either side of the memorial are two benches, not just for sitting but in honor of those who survived the massacre.

The Government Response

The day after the massacre, President George W. Bush and his wife arrived to attend the convocation at the Tech. All who were affected by the tragedy were granted extensions of up to six months by the Internal Revenue Service and the Virginia Department of taxation. Governor Tim Kaine had been on a trade mission in Japan, but after hearing the news of the shootings, he returned early and declared a state of emergency. By doing so, it enabled him to deploy any equipment, personnel or other resources immediately.

Later the Governor created a panel of eight members to review everything related to the massacre, including the delayed warning to the students by the school, the time it took to lock down the campus, and Cho's medical and mental health history. By August 2007, the panel had reached their conclusions about the incident, and these included twenty major findings. They found the Virginia Tech Police Department did 'not take sufficient action to deal with what might happen if the initial lead proved erroneous'. More than 70 recommendations were made to colleges, universities, law enforcement officials, emergency service providers, mental health providers, public officials and law makers, to help prevent this type of tragedy from recurring.

Regardless of the faults, flaws and errors in the procedures and judgments made on that day, the panel concluded that ultimately the blame lay solely on Cho. He was responsible for his own actions, and there could be no blame laid upon anyone else. It was also concluded that the death toll could have been lower if the university had made a decision immediately to cancel all classes after the discovery of the first two bodies. The university also should have sent a warning out to all students immediately that there was potentially a gunman still on campus.

Cho's rampage also had an effect on the state and federal gun purchasing laws. Gaps were discovered in the laws surrounding firearms and officials were appointed to examine what those gaps were and how to close them. An executive order was made by Governor Kaine to close the gaps. Because of this event, the first gun control law in more than ten years was passed. This bill instated reporting improvements to the National Instant Criminal Background Check System (NICS) to prevent criminals and those declared mentally ill from purchasing firearms. On January 5, 2008, the measure was signed by President Bush.

Response by the Academic Industry

Throughout North America, hundreds of universities and colleges joined with Virginia Tech in conducting memorial services and vigils. Cash donations were offered by some schools, and additional counseling support for the faculty and students at Virginia Tech was offered. The biggest effect this tragedy had was it caused other universities to have a good look at their own safety and security procedures on campus as well as the mental health support services that were provided.

The Legal Aftermath

Twenty-four victims' families brought forward a lawsuit against the state of Virginia, and on June 17, 2008, Judge Markow approved a settlement worth $11 million. This settlement was also for the 18 victims who were injured, and their needs for lifelong health care were included. Of those not included in this settlement, two families decided not to file claims, and two were unresolved.

The university was fined $55,000 by the Department of Education for failing to notify the students of the danger fast enough after the first two shootings. It was the highest fine that could be imposed. The university appealed the decision. The decision was overturned on March 30, 2012, by a federal judge who determined the Tech had not violated the Clery Act. The understanding of the initial two shootings was that it was likely a domestic incident; therefore, the university was unaware there was still a very real risk to their students and faculty members. However, in September the Education Secretary reversed the decision again, this time imposing a fine of $27,500. They were then fined an additional $5,000 in January 2014. Eventually, unable to continue fighting, Virginia Tech paid $32,500 in fines in February 2014. They made a statement that although they didn't agree with the fines, it was time to put it to rest for the sake of the community as well as the financial impact.

The parents of two students killed that day had opted to file a wrongful death civil suit against the Tech rather than join in with those families on the settlement. Initially on March 14, 2012, the Tech was found guilty of negligence for delaying the warning. However, in October 2013, the Virginia Supreme Court reversed this decision, stating 'there was no duty for the Commonwealth to warn students about the potential for criminal acts by third parties'. The state claimed that Cho was the only person responsible for what happened that day.

Cho's Writings

Play – Richard McBeef

Cho had written a short one-act play in 2006 called Richard McBeef. The main character and story revolved around a 13-year-old boy called John, who had lost his father to a boating accident, and his stepfather Richard McBeef who was an ex-football player. Throughout the play, John referred to Richard as 'Dick'. Richard tried to have a father-to-son talk with John and touches his lap, and the boy quickly claims he is being molested by his stepfather. He then accuses Richard of killing John's biological father and states repeatedly that he will kill Richard. A major argument then takes place between Richard, John and John's mother Sue. Richard goes out to his car to get away from the conflict, and John follows him and harasses him in the car. At the end of the play, John is trying to shove a banana-flavored cereal bar into Richard's throat. Richard, who is supposed to be passive, reacts 'out of sheer desecrated hurt and anger' by 'swinging a deadly blow' at John.

Play – Mr. Brownstone

This play was another Cho had written for a class assignment. In this story, there are three 17-year- olds called John, Jane and Joe, who are sitting in a casino discussing their deep hatred towards their 45-year-old mathematics teacher, Mr. Brownstone. The three teens claim (by using the term 'ass-rape') they are mistreated by Mr. Brownstone. John then wins a jackpot on a slot machine worth multi-millions, and Mr. Brownstone, despite volleys of profanity coming from the teens, reports that they are underage to the casino officials. Mr. Brownstone then claims the winning ticket was his and the teens had taken it from him. One whole page in this play contains the lyrics to the song "Mr. Brownstone" by Guns N' Roses, which was written about heroin.

Fiction Paper

Around one year before he went on the deadly rampage, Cho wrote a paper for an Intro to Short Fiction class assignment. This paper was written about a mass school murder that the protagonist of the story had planned, but in the story he did not follow through with the plan. The Virginia Tech panel did not know this paper existed, but when information about the paper surfaced, the panel learned that the only people who had copies of the paper were the Virginia State Police and Virginia Tech. The police claimed they hadn't handed over the paper to the panel because they were prevented from doing so by law as it was part of an ongoing investigation.

However, Virginia Tech had known about the existence of the paper, and school officials had even discussed it after the shootings. Governor Kaine stated the Tech was expected to hand over all of Cho's writings to the panel. Eventually Virginia Tech gave the panel a copy of the paper. The exact contents of this paper have never been released to the public.

Timeline of the Massacre

5:00 am

Cho's roommate notices that Cho is awake and seated in front of his computer in their suite.

5:30 am

Another roommate saw Cho putting acne cream on his face and brushing his teeth.

5:30 am – 6:00 am

Roommate saw Cho get dressed, then leave the room.

Before 7:00 am

Cho is seen standing outside the entrance to West Ambler Johnston Hall.

Before 7:15 am

Emily Hilscher is dropped off at her dormitory, West Ambler Johnston, by her boyfriend.

7:15 am

Campus police receive a 9-1-1 call reporting a shooting at West Ambler Johnston Hall. Ryan Clark is deceased and Emily Hilscher fatally injured.

7:15 am – 9:01 am

Cho goes back to his room and leaves a note.

7:30 am

Virginia Tech Police Department and Blacksburg Police Department investigators arrive.

7:30 am – 8:00 am

Hilscher's friend and roommate Heather Haugh returns to the building and is questioned by detectives. She explains Hilscher usually stays at her boyfriend's house on the weekends and he drops her off on Monday mornings before he travels on to Radford University where he is studying. She also tells police Hilscher's boyfriend is an avid user of guns.

8:00 am

Classes begin.

Around 8:00 am

West Ambler Johnston is locked down. Resident assistant on the third floor notifies students.

8:25 am

Leadership team of Virginia Tech meets to plan how to let students know about the homicides. Police locate Hilscher's boyfriend and he is detained for questioning.

8:52 am

The office of the University President, Charles Steger, is locked down.

9:00 am

Leadership team briefed on the homicide investigation.

9:01 am

Cho mails an express parcel from the Blacksburg Post Office to the NBC headquarters in New York. Parcel contains a manifesto, photographs and video clips pertaining to the massacre that is about to take place.

9:05 am

The Intermediate French class in Norris 211 begins.

9:05 am – 9:15 am

Cho is seen in Norris Hall blocking the doors with chains from the inside.

9:26 am

Emails are sent to the students, faculty and campus staff informing them of the homicide earlier.

9:30 am

A female student enters Norris 211 and tells everyone about the homicide in West Ambler Johnston earlier.

9:42 am

A 9-1-1 call is made by students in Norris Hall that shots are being fired.

9:45 am

Police arrive and find the doors chained up.

9:40 am – 9:51 am

Cho starts shooting and strikes 47 people, killing 30. The whole rampage lasted for around nine minutes. This is known because a student noted the time when the shooting started.

Around 9:40 am

Students in Norris 205 hear the gunshots and barricade the door.

9:50 am

It takes the police five minutes to gather their team together and clear the area before they can break down the doors. A shotgun is used to break through the chains. It is believed Cho heard the noise and realized the police were gaining entry. Cho is still shooting, so the police follow the sounds up to the second floor.

9:50 am

A second email is sent out warning there is a gunman on the loose and to stay inside buildings until told it is safe to leave. Recipients are also told to avoid windows. The Tech's loudspeakers also broadcast this information.

9:51 am

As police reach the second floor, Cho stops shooting. It is then discovered that Cho has committed suicide by shooting himself in the temple.

10:17 am

A third email is sent advising all classes are cancelled and everyone should stay put.

10:52 am

Fourth email sent stating there had been a multiple shooting and there were multiple victims in Norris Hall. It mistakenly says the shooter has been arrested and police were searching for a possible second assailant. The entrances to all of the buildings on campus are locked.

12:00 pm

A press conference is held and authorities advise there may be more than 21 people killed and 28 injured.

12:42 pm

University President announces people are being released from the buildings by police and they were setting up counseling centers.

From Childhood to Death

Cho Seung-Hui was a deeply disturbed individual, and the evidence to support this theory is there in the transcripts of his childhood. As a child, it was obvious to his family, teachers and doctors that something was very wrong with Cho. He was seen on numerous occasions by mental health specialists, and received diagnoses and therapies that were supposed to help him grow into a regular adult. But despite the efforts of everyone around him, the treatments just weren't enough.

To his parents' credit, they did everything they possibly could to find out what was wrong with Cho as a child, and even as a young adult, they were still trying to get him the help they felt he needed. At one point he was even hospitalized and treated, but even that wasn't enough to prevent what was going to happen. There hadn't been any serious concerns that Cho would hurt others, however. He had been cautioned over a couple of cases of stalking, but there was nothing indicating he was a physical threat.

Unfortunately we have seen over again the effects bullying can have on a child, particularly one that is struggling to fit in to the 'normal' lanes of school. Those like Cho that are quiet, lonesome, non-communicative, become targets in the schoolyard for being different, and this escalates those feelings of worthlessness, anger, frustration and hatred. Some children go on to overcome these things, but others, like Cho, continue to have it festering in the recesses of their mind for years to come.

Killers who enter schools and open fire on the students and faculty members are often children who were bullied at school. Cho felt he could relate to killers such as Dylan Klebold and Eric Harris, the Columbine shooters. He saw in them the same thoughts and feelings he was having himself. He believed that he had been the victim of terrible wrongdoings throughout his life, and he was determined to seek some sort of 'revenge' and to make himself heard.

His difficulties in communicating with speech would have aggravated his feelings of being ignored or not listened to. He was incapable of speaking up and telling people how he really felt. Until it was too late. Then, he made multiple videos of himself, rambling tales of conspiracy and hatred, and he wrote a manifesto that barely made sense to anyone who read it after his death.

Cho entered Virginia Tech that day determined to take as many lives as he possibly could. He had planned it, and set up the first murders as a distraction. He was calm, calculated, and willing to lose his own life that day. Like with many cases, the warning signs were there that something was going to go terribly wrong with Cho. His teachers, family, fellow students, and the faculty, all saw him spiraling out of control. But nobody was able to do anything to prevent him from committing one of the deadliest school rampages.

CHAPTER 6:

George Hennard – The Luby's Massacre

On October 16, 1991, a man by the name of George Hennard purposely drove his pickup truck through the front of a restaurant called Luby's Cafeteria in Killeen, Texas. But destroying the front of the restaurant wasn't his only intention that day. It simply provided him with an easy way to gain access on a grand scale, because what he was planning on doing was far worse than any of the diners that day could have imagined.

From Navy Man to Murderer

Georges Pierre Hennard was born on October 15, 1956, in Pennsylvania. He would later be known as George Jo Hennard, and his father was a surgeon born in Switzerland, and his mother took care of the home and the children. They would go on to have two more children – Alan and Desiree. From the age of five years, Hennard and his family began shifting from place to place as his father worked for different Army hospitals across the country. At one point they lived in New Mexico as his father was working at the White Sands Missile Range near Las Cruces.

Hennard was quite popular at school because the other kids

thought he was good looking and cool. He had an outgoing personality, and everyone seemed to look up to him. He was even nicknamed Jo-Jo while he was at school. But this seemingly happy child would soon change completely after an incident involving his father, and his life would end up taking a very different path.

Hennard's father was known to be tough, and one year the father and son got into an awful fight. Hennard went to school the next day with his hair cut so badly it looked as though it had been done with a butcher's knife. This turned the outgoing Hennard into an introverted teen, and he was never the same again. He ended up keeping to himself right through high school, a complete loner, and he certainly didn't talk or associate with any girls. It seemed his parents didn't care, and they weren't around much anyway.

Following his high school graduation in 1974, Hennard enlisted with the Navy. He completed three years before being honorably discharged, and he later signed up to work with Merchant Marines. This involved him largely working in the Gulf of Mexico, and in 1981, he started the first of his overseas voyages, completing 37 in total. However, the more he traveled, the worse trouble he seemed to find.

In 1981 he was caught in Texas with marijuana in his possession. The following year, he reportedly got involved in a racial argument with one of his shipmates, and this resulted in him having his seaman's papers suspended. An acquaintance later stated Hennard hated blacks, gays and Hispanics, and women were nothing more than snakes. His feelings towards women worsened each time he had an argument with his mother.

Hennard lost his seaman's license again in 1989, once again being caught with marijuana in his possession. He subsequently enrolled in a program for drug abuse. He started to drift from a variety of jobs, and ended up living with his mother for a while in the large colonial home she kept after divorcing Hennard's father. The home, located in Belton, was constructed with red brick.

By February 1991, Hennard was starting to exhibit some bizarre behavior. He had managed to purchase two weapons – a Glock 17 and a Ruger P89, but it is unknown whether he was planning ahead or simply liked the weapons. In June of that year, Hennard sent a five-page letter to two sisters that lived nearby. He apparently admired the girls, and asked in the letter if the three of them could get together some day. He also wrote, "please give me the satisfaction of someday laughing in the face of all those mostly white tremendously female vipers...who tried to destroy me and my family."

Less than two weeks before he carried out his plan at Luby's, Hennard had collected his paycheck from a job he had been working at and then quit. He was heard asking himself what would happen if he was to kill someone. One of his work colleagues at the time later stated Hennard kept saying 'watch and see, watch and see'. He had talked about some women in Belton whom he perceived had been giving him problems.

October 15 was his birthday, and after speaking to his mother by phone, he went to a small restaurant for dinner. While there, the television was showing coverage of Clarence Thomas's confirmation hearings, and Hennard flew into a rage, especially during an interview with a woman called Anita Hall. According to the restaurant manager, Hennard began screaming and calling the woman a dumb bitch. He shouted that the 'bastards opened the door for all the women!'

Luby's Cafeteria Massacre

The day after his birthday, on October 16, Hennard went to the same convenience store he went to every morning for his regular breakfast of junk food. This had been his routine for over a year, and staff always remembered him as a brooding man who had a sense of hostility in his eyes. He was usually in a hurry, but this morning things were different. The cashier that handled his purchases thought he was almost friendly and calm for a change, and she had never seen him like that before.

Seven hours later, Hennard rammed the front of the Luby's Cafeteria with his Ford Ranger pickup truck during the lunchtime period. The front windows of the building shattered as the truck drove straight into the restaurant. At first, patrons likely thought it was simply a car accident, until they saw Hennard get out of the truck with guns in his hands. Hennard then opened fire, first with the Glock and later with the Ruger. There were around 80 people inside at the time, including the staff.

As he moved around the cafeteria shooting at people, he at one point let a mother and her 4-year- old child leave. For those who witnessed the massacre, it seemed as though Hennard was picking and choosing his victims rather than firing randomly at everyone who was there. The women appeared to be the main targets, and he shouted out that all women of Killeen and Belton were vipers, and 'see what you've done to me and my family!' He repeatedly asked, 'Is it worth it? Tell me, is it worth it?'

Those inside the cafeteria quickly ducked and hid beneath the chairs, benches and tables. Some were praying, their hands clasped with others. Nobody seemed to be panicking, and there was a strange sense of calm and silence in between Hennard's shouts and gunfire. Not one person made a rush for the door. Sam Wink, 47, happened to be there that day as he and his work colleagues were shouting their boss lunch for National Bosses' Day.

When the truck crashed through the building, Wink jumped into the aisle, and then heard sounds like the popping of light bulbs. It turned out those sounds were gunfire, as Hennard started shooting from inside the cab of his truck. When he got out, he systematically shot the customers who were waiting at the service counters for their lunch. Hennard took his time circling the Cafeteria, calmly choosing his victims. He glared at a woman, called her a bitch, and then shot her dead. Another woman who was hiding under a bench was his next target. He asked her if she was hiding, called her a bitch, and shot her to death as well. At one point Hennard turned around and, for a second, his eyes met with Wink's. He had a smirk on his face, but his eyes were very mean. Wink was surprised at how his eyes could look so intense and angry, yet his face showed calmness, even when he was shouting.

His calm expression was also noticed by Dr. Shawn Isdale, a chiropractor, who was at the Cafeteria with his wife and daughter and his parents. There was no emotion displayed on his face, and he seemed strangely composed and relaxed. A friend of Dr. Isdale's, Steve Ernst, was hiding underneath a table when Hennard walked up to him and shot him. He then shot Ernst's wife, striking her in the arm, but the bullet went straight through her and struck Venice Ellen Henehan, who was Ernst's mother-in-law, and she was killed.

When Hennard paused to reload his weapons, there was complete silence in the Cafeteria. Nobody said a word, as though they were either waiting for him to shoot them or perhaps they thought if they were quiet he wouldn't notice them. One of the diners, an auto mechanic called Tommy Vaughan, was certain he was next when he saw Hennard move towards the table he was under. Vaughan was a large man, standing 6 ft. 6 in. and weighing 300 lbs., and rather than being shot, he threw his body through the window beside him. Almost immediately, scores of people were trying to make a run for the window to escape. The police arrived a few minutes later, and by then almost a third of the diners had managed to get out.

Once the police officers made their way into the restaurant and engaged Hennard, a volley of gunshots went back and forth between them. Hennard was shot three times and retreated to an alcove at the back of the restaurant, where he subsequently shot and killed himself.

Twenty-Three Victims

There were 50 victims in total, with 23 killed and 27 wounded. All of those killed were adults, and their names are as follows:

James Walter Welsh – (75) – Waco, Texas

Lula Belle Welsh – (64) – Waco Texas

Zona Mae Lynn – (45) – Austin, Texas

Thomas Earl Simmons – (55) – Killeen, Texas

Olgica Andonovsk Taylor – (45) – Waco, Texas

Iva Juanita Williams – (64) – Temple, Texas

Nancy Faye Stansbury – (44) – Harker Heights, Texas

John Raymond Romero Jr. – (33) – Copperas Cove, Texas

Glen Arval Spivey – (44) – Harker Heights, Texas

Ruth Marie Pujol – (36) – Copperas Cove, Texas

Su-zan Neal Rashott – (30) – San Antonio, Texas

Sylvia Mathilde King – (64) – Marlin, Texas

Connie Dean Peterson – (55) – Austin, Texas

Dr. Michael Edward Griffith – (48) – Copperas Cove, Texas

Clodine Delphia Humphrey – (63) – Killeen, Texas

Debra Ann Gray – (33) – Copperas Cove, Texas

Venice Ellen Henehan – (70) – Metz, Missouri

Al Gratia – (71) – Copperas Cove, Texas

Ursula Edith Marie Gratia – (67) – Copperas Cove, Texas

Jimmie Eugene Caruthers – (48) – Austin, Texas

Lt. Col. Steven Charles Dody – (43) – Fort Hood, Texas

Kriemhild A. Davis – (62) – Killeen, Texas

Patricia Brawn Carney – (57) – Belton, Texas

Police Immediate Response

At the Sheridan Hotel just two buildings down from Luby's, an auto theft prevention seminar was taking place, and attending were five Texan law enforcement officers, including an officer of the Killeen Police Department. Also in the immediate vicinity were two undercover officers who were working an assignment. When the urgent call for assistance was broadcast all seven of the officers rushed to the scene.

On arrival, three officers made entry into the building straight away, as the other four formed a perimeter. It's important to note that back then there was no training for police officers to manage an active shooter. The officers couldn't wait, as they knew people were dying inside the restaurant. Once inside, an officer placed himself near the entrance. The other two officers separated with one going down each side of the building interior. Hennard was still shooting at people and was unaware the police officers had entered.

The officers then aggressively fired upon Hennard, and he was shot three times. This made him stop what he was doing immediately, and he ran towards the back of the restaurant. There was an alcove in the back near the restrooms, and Hennard moved into the alcove. It was here that Hennard put an end to his massacre by shooting himself in the head.

A Man Who Hated Women

Hennard had a clear hatred of women, though why that is remains uncertain. He was known to have furious fights with his mother, and he used to draw cartoon caricatures of her but with a snake's body. He had at one point threatened to kill his mother, yet would end up living with her from time to time. It seems to be a common thread with many serial killers to have an issue with their mothers. Hennard also preferred to listen to music that had lyrics which expressed violence towards women. He had been known to refer to women as disgusting and vile creatures.

The majority of Hennard's victims were women, and given he was seen to be carefully choosing who he shot that day, it's reasonable to assume that the female gender were his ultimate targets. As mentioned earlier, Hennard had once sent a letter to Jana Jernigan, 19, and her sister Jill Fritz, 23, in June. The letter was five pages long, and his rambling words seem to depict he had a fantasy relationship with the sisters. One part of the letter read: 'it is very ironic about Belton, Texas. I found the best and worst in women there. You and your sister are the one side. Then the abundance of evil women that make up the worst on the other side…I will no matter what prevail over the female vipers in those two rinky-dink towns in Texas. I will prevail in the end'.

The mother of the sisters felt uneasy when she read the letter, and she took it to the police station to see what they made of it, but she barely got a response. Her husband happened to be the administrator of a hospital in Tennessee, so she got him to take a look at it. He then showed a staff psychiatrist who stated the letter showed the writer had an obsessive infatuation with the two sisters. The psychiatrist felt the letter indicated Hennard carried a lot of humiliation and anger with him and he could be dangerous.

Why Did He Finally Snap?

The answer to that question remains unknown, but there have been plenty of theories and assumptions made to date. Many experts believe it was a combination of Hennard's social isolation, feelings of rejection, and a long-standing rage against women and the world. After the massacre, the investigation that followed indicated Hennard fit the profile of a mass murderer.

Hennard had a muscular physique and was considered a handsome man, the type women would have found attractive. He lived in a very nice house, with gardens that were kept immaculate. Even by birth, Hennard fit into a higher class due to his father being a surgeon. However, he was still a loner and some would say a loser. During the months of February and March 1991, Hennard had spent some time in Nevada with his mother. It was here that he bought the weapons he needed to carry out his massacre. Purchasing the weapons may have been triggered by the rejection he received in February declining to reinstate him in the Merchant Marines.

Hennard had obviously been thinking about killing for quite a while, considering he had put some level of planning into what he was going to do and where. He had asked one of his co-workers a month beforehand what he should do if he was to kill somebody. His co-worker replied that if he killed someone, then he should kill himself. Not long after this conversation, Hennard tried to sell his guns but was unable to.

A former roommate told a reporter that Hennard had talked about killing himself before. Hennard's reasons were because he had no girlfriends or friends, and he had no respect for his mother. While the two shared a home, the roommate worked at night stocking grocery shelves, and Hennard would get up at the crack of dawn each morning. He would then proceed to turn the television on or turn the stereo up, without considering his poor roommate trying to sleep.

Most of those who had come into contact with Hennard over the years thought of him as rude, troubled, combative and a loner. Hennard seemed unable to form relationships with people, and he was considered obnoxious when he drank alcohol. Everything seemed to really unravel for Hennard when he lost his seaman's papers. Working on the sea was the only job Hennard ever seemed to enjoy, yet his colleagues were glad to see him go. He was argumentative and loud, and he always had the kind of cold look in his eyes that made his work colleagues uncomfortable.

Following the massacre, police investigations discovered Hennard had an almost obsessive interest in serial killers. He also was obsessed with a song, 'Don't Take Me Alive', by rock band Steely Dan. The lyrics are about a criminal in a last stand against law enforcement. The record store owner who sold Hennard the album felt he couldn't cope with his place in life. He believed Hennard desired to be remembered for something, regardless of what it may be.

A calendar from 1989 was found at Hennard's home, and he had written various remarks on it. One of these included: 'They shall live with what they have created and they shall find no redemption in what they have done'. The last remark written on the calendar was 'There is simply no hope and not a prayer'. Two video tapes were also found amongst his belongings, one of which was a documentary on the Lockerbie bombing in 1987. The other was a documentary on mass murderers and serial killers, including James Huberty. It appeared Hennard had been researching massacres and mass murder for many months before he joined the ranks of those he studied.

Aftermath

The community was quick to leap into action following the massacre, comforting those that had lost loved ones and those that had survived but were injured. Staff at the local hospital worked tirelessly managing those with injuries, and local pastors worked just as hard to comfort their parishioners. The local police delved into every aspect of Hennard's life, trying to find out what his motive could have been. They determined factors that influenced Hennard were his drug use, misogyny and his unhappy personal life.

Local gun laws were also changed following the Luby's massacre. In 1995, Texas passed a 'shall issue' law that meant all applicants who qualified would be issued a Concealed Handgun License, but they must pass the criteria as per the law. Although a Concealed Handgun License is mandatory in Texas, this new law meant discretion would be removed from the issuing authority. In other words, if the applicant met the legal criteria, a license would be issued automatically.

This criterion, however, is strict. If any of the mandatory tests are failed, the license would be denied. Applicants had to have a clean criminal record, have attended ten hours or more of classes with an instructor who was state certified, pass a test made up of 50 questions, pass two background checks and pass a shooting test of 50 rounds. Suzanna Hupp, one of the survivors of Hennard's massacre had strongly campaigned for the law change. She even went on to serve in the Texas House of Representatives under the Republicans from 1997 to 2006.

A memorial to those who had been killed and injured at Luby's that day was constructed behind the Community Center, which is near the site where Luby's used to stand. It was made of pink granite and carries the names of those who lost their lives and the date of the massacre.

Following Hennard's rampage that day, the building was repaired and cleaned thoroughly and reopened for business. It was never the same though, and business had dropped dramatically. The restaurant was redesigned, but despite the best efforts of the owners, it was closed down in September 2000. It would later become a Chinese-American buffet restaurant.

Survivors Tell

The Rev. Kirby Lack was meeting his friend Michael Griffith for lunch and had just sat down at their table. Griffith had received news about his finances earlier and felt he needed to console himself with his friend's company and some dessert. Lack had even been making morose jokes about his funeral, to which Lack told him he was his friend and he loved him, which wasn't something Lack would normally say.

According to Lack, when Hennard got out of his truck, he walked around it three times, shooting the whole time. Lack was lying on the floor, trying to remain still, but Hennard still shot him in the lower part of this back. He even pressed the gun barrel up against Lack's head, but miraculously when he fired, he missed and it hit the floor just inches away. It was then the police officers arrived on the scene. One memory that stayed with Lack was the look in Hennard's eyes as he drove into the building. His eyes were huge and resembled egg whites from a distance.

Suzanna Hupp (nee Gratia) was friends with the manager of the restaurant, and on that day he invited her to come for lunch, but she was busy so she said no. But then her parents, Al and Ursula, turned up and also asked her to come to Luby's for lunch. She decided to give in and go. They went to Luby's often and had a regular table, but this time they decided to sit somewhere else. The manager, Mark Koppenhaffe, joined them for lunch.

As they were finishing their meals, Koppenhaffe left and went back to the kitchen just as the truck came crashing through. The Gratias took cover as soon as the shooting began, and Hupp remembered her pistol was not in her purse but in her car. Laws at the time prevented her from carrying it at all times. Her father Al, despite his age, made a charge towards Hennard. He had managed to travel half the distance between them before being shot in the chest.

Meanwhile, Tommy Vaughn had been throwing himself repeatedly against a window at the back of the restaurant, determined to break it. Fortunately the glass had been weakened by a bullet, and the glass shattered. Many of those people inside saw the opportunity and made a run for the window, with up to 50 making it outside. Hupp raced towards the window as well, shouting for her mother to follow her.

It wasn't until she had made it outside that Hupp realized her mother hadn't come out the window. Later, law enforcement officers explained that her mother had been shot in the head by Hennard as she comforted her husband. Both her parents had been killed.

A Rampage Based on Hate

George Hennard was torn between needing his mother and hating the female species. He would fight and argue with his mother and threaten to kill her, then go and live with her for periods of time. He spoke to his mother on his birthday, yet the following day would declare to everyone in the Luby's cafeteria how much he hated women. It appears he never had a serious girlfriend or a wife, so where this hatred came from isn't overly clear.

The incident when his father hacked off his hair and sent him to school was a major turning point for a number of reasons. The teasing and bullying Hennard would have endured at that time must have been horrendous. It's no wonder he wouldn't talk to girls at school. Perhaps that fear of humiliation followed him into adulthood. After all, the letter he sent to two girls in the neighborhood is a bit of a strange way for an adult to try and strike up some sort of dialogue with the opposite sex. Most men would call or approach, but he was only comfortable with sending a five-page letter.

During his rampage, Hennard claimed women were snakes and had destroyed his family, but nobody knows what he meant by that.

When his victims were examined following the shootings, it was clear that they were predominantly women. Witnesses on that day even claimed to have seen him singling out the females in the cafeteria to shoot. There was obviously something buried in his brain that women were the cause of all of his problems. But why?

Many of his associates and colleagues over the years knew Hennard had deep beliefs regarding women, and he also had a distaste for other ethnicities, such as Hispanics. It was considered he chose that particular restaurant because of its proximity to the border of Mexico, as if he believed the restaurant would be full of Hispanics. But it is more likely he chose a place he knew would have a high percentage of female patrons at that time of the day.

Another contributing factor leading up to that fateful day, was his rejection from the Merchant Marines. He wanted to be back to sea, probably because he would be surrounded by men, as women weren't common sailors in those days. The only time he seemed to be happy in life was while he was at sea. Perhaps it was the isolation and distance he felt from his mother and father. Far from the mother that fought with him, and the father who humiliated him.

On the day that Hennard drove his truck through the windows of Luby's then opened fire on those inside is quite likely the day he truly lost his mind. He was prepared for the onslaught and had put a lot of thought into it. Some would say it was a blessing that he died that day, but in some ways it is a shame, because now we'll never know what went wrong with George Hennard.

CHAPTER 7:
Kenneth Bianchi and Angelo Buono –
The Hillside Stranglers

Perhaps one of the more obscure type of killers, Bianchi and Buono worked together to torture and kill women in Los Angeles over the period of a year, between 1977 and 1978. Serial killers almost always work alone, but this was not the case with the Hillside Stranglers. The naked bodies of prostitutes were found dumped on hillsides in the city, but it wasn't until women who were not prostitutes started turning up dead that the attention of the media and the public heightened. Once captured, authorities were surprised to find Bianchi and Buono were related to each other, and their trials would become the most expensive in the history of California law at that time.

Kindred Cousins

On May 22, 1951, Kenneth Alessio Bianchi was born to a 17-year-old prostitute who was also an alcoholic, and he was immediately given up for adoption. Nicholas Bianchi and Frances Sciolono adopted the baby and provided him with a stable upbringing.

However, as a child he would become a pathological liar, and he spent much of his time daydreaming instead of doing what he was meant to be doing. Doctors would later diagnose these daydreaming episodes as a form of epilepsy, called petit mal seizures. During these periods, his eyes would roll back and he would be unresponsive. As part of the investigation into his seizures, doctors also determined Bianchi suffered from a passive-aggressive personality disorder. He was also a frequent bed wetter and did not do well at school despite having a good IQ.

In 1957, Bianchi had an accidental fall from a jungle gym and, for some reason, his mother thought he needed to go to a Catholic school to try and change his behaviors. Later, in 1963, Bianchi had a sudden urge to pull down the pants of a six-year- old girl and discovered he liked doing it. Unfortunately his father passed away the following year, and Bianchi was taken out of the expensive private Catholic school and sent to the public high school. He was popular with the girls there, and after he graduated in 1971, he married Brenda Beck, his high school sweetheart. The marriage was not to last, though, and they divorced after just 8 months together.

Bianchi then decided he wanted to become a police officer, and started studying psychology and police science at the Community College. This didn't last either, though, and he dropped out of the program after only one semester. He still put in an application with the local sheriff's department but failed. From there he took on a variety of jobs, one of which was as a security guard at a jewelry store. Unfortunately Bianchi couldn't help himself and started stealing from the store and giving the jewelry away to his girlfriends which resulted in him being fired.

In 1975 Bianchi moved away to stay with his cousin in California. Angelo Buono was 17 years older than Bianchi, and he showed him how to get free sex from prostitutes by flashing a fake police badge. For a while, the two men became pimps, but the girls they hired ran away, so that venture failed. Bianchi hadn't given up the idea of being a police officer and would apply at different departments but was never successful. He eventually started working at a title company, and when he got his first check, he used it to get a Cadillac and an apartment. He met a woman through work called Kelli Boyd, and the two settled into the apartment together. She became pregnant in 1977, which prompted Bianchi to propose, but she declined. They still continued to live together, though.

Angelo Buono was born on October 5, 1934, to Italian immigrants living in Rochester, New York. His parents divorced when he was young, and at the age of 5, he moved with his mother and sister to Glendale, California. As he got older, Buono seemed to have a very high interest in sex, and as a teenager he would brag about raping girls. Disturbingly Buono idolized Caryl Chessman, the 'Red Light Bandit', who was a serial rapist. Buono saw Chessman as his hero but felt the rapist should have murdered his victims as well.

Buono began to steal cars, and when he was caught, he was put into reform school. He would later marry his high school sweetheart, Geraldine Vinal, who at 17 was pregnant, but he walked away from the marriage just a week later. The baby boy was born in early 1956, but his father would not pay any child support and divorced his mother. Buono would go on to marry a second time, to Mary Castillo, and they would eventually have five children together.

Allegations were made in 1964 that Buono had raped his daughter Grace who was only 2 years old at the time. Very little information was made available and no charges were ever laid. The marriage reached an end soon after and they divorced that same year. Castillo made further allegations that Buono was sexually and physically abusive towards her, yet she did try to reconcile with him at one point. But when he placed her in handcuffs and pointed a gun at her, she soon changed her mind.

In 1965 Buono found himself with a third wife, Nannette Campino, who was a single mother at the time. Two children were born into this union, and after being arrested for stealing cars again, Buono was sentenced to serve a year in prison. But because he had such a big family to support, the court suspended the sentence. This marriage also ended in divorce, and under similar circumstances, with reports of sexual and physical abuse and the rape of their daughter.

Buono seemed to be very appealing to women, and he married

again in 1972 to Deborah Taylor, but the couple never lived under the same roof. During this marriage, Buono was also dating a teenager who got pregnant twice, and he would often force other women to perform oral sex on him. Once Bianchi moved in with him, it was easy for the two men to share their ideas and fantasies regarding the rape and murder of women.

Sexual Abuse, Torture, Death

As pimps, Buono and Bianchi had two girls working for them who were more or less held captive by the men. Buono inflicted horrible abuse on both women, and as soon as they were able, they escaped. Bianchi wasn't happy because he liked having the extra income, so they managed to find another girl to work for them. But they needed more punters, so they purchased a trick list with names of those who frequently used prostitutes from Deborah Noble, herself a prostitute, and her friend Yolanda Washington.

Yolanda Washington

During the trick list exchange, Yolanda had told Buono that when she worked, it was always on a particular stretch of Sunset Boulevard. So when the two men discovered the list was fake and they couldn't find Deborah, Yolanda became the target of their rage. At just 19 years old, Yolanda was found naked and dead on a hillside near Ventura Freeway on October 18, 1977. Her body showed faint marks around the ankles, wrists and neck, which indicated she had been tied up before her death. She had been raped, and her body had been cleaned before it was left in plain sight on the hillside.

Judy Miller

Around November 1, 1977, another body of a young girl was found in similar circumstances as Yolanda. She was naked, and there were marks on her ankles, wrists and neck. She too had been tied up, and it appeared she had also been strangled to death. She was lying on a parkway, face upwards, her legs positioned in the shape of a diamond, and had been dumped there by her killer. Her autopsy showed she had been sodomized and raped, and a tiny piece of fluff was collected from her eyelid for later forensic analysis. She was identified as 15-year-old Judy Miller, a runaway.

Elissa Kastin

Within five days of the discovery of Judy's body, another naked body was found. Like the others, she also had the same marks indicating she had been bound. She was lying near the Chevy Chase Country Club, and was later identified as Elissa 'Lissa' Kastin, 21, who worked as a dancer, waitress, and sometimes a prostitute. Her autopsy showed she had been raped and strangled.

Jill Barcomb

On November 9, Jill Barcomb's naked body was found near Beverly Hills. An 18-year-old prostitute, Jill's body had the same markings as the others. By now the police were coming to the conclusion they had a serial killer operating in the area, but because the victims had been runaways or prostitutes, there was very little interest in the media. There was no political drive either to address the situation.

Kathleen Robinson

November 18 saw the addition to the increasing number of dead women of Kathleen Robinson, who was a 17-year-old high school student. Like the others, she was naked when found and had been tied up and raped.

Attempted Murder – Catharine Lorre

In early November, two men pulled over Catharine Lorre and showed her their police badges, asking for her identification. Catharine was the daughter of a famous actor, Peter Lorre, who ironically had been made famous by playing a serial killer in the film 'M', and when she handed her identification to the 'police officers', they noticed a photo of her sitting in Peter Lorre's lap. Realizing who she was and the media attention it would draw, they let her go.

Dolores Cepeda and Sonja Johnson

Dolores Ann 'Dolly' Cepeda, 12, and Sonja Marie Johnson, 14, were last seen getting off a school bus on November 13. Witnesses saw the girls approach a sedan with two men sitting inside. Seven days later, their bodies were found by a young boy who had been looking for treasure in a trash heap. They were on a hillside close to Dodger Stadium, and both were already beginning to decompose. However, the autopsy was able to show that both girls had been raped and strangled.

Kristina Weckler

The same day as the two girls were found, another body was found on a hillside between Eagle Rock and Glendale. Hikers had discovered the naked body of Kristina Weckler, 20, and the usual ligature marks were visible on her ankles, wrists and neck. This time, her body showed bruises on her breasts, and she had blood oozing from her anus. Another difference from the other bodies was that Kristina had two puncture marks on her arm, but she was not a drug user. Much later it would be discovered she had been injected with a cleaning agent called Windex.

Evelyn Jane King

Although she had gone missing sometime around November 9, the decomposed body of 28-year- old actress Evelyn was not found until November 23. She was found off the Golden State Freeway near the Los Feliz off-ramp. The decomposition was so bad that it was impossible to tell if she had been tortured or raped, but the autopsy did indicate she had been strangled just like the other murdered women. Finally a task force was created to catch the killer who was now known as the 'Hillside Strangler'.

Lauren Wagner

Lauren Wagner, 18, was a business student who was living with her parents in San Fernando Valley when she disappeared. She didn't come home one night, and her car was found opposite the house with the door open the following morning. A neighbor had actually seen Lauren get abducted by two men, and heard Lauren shout out while she was being taken. Her body was found on November 29 in the hills near Mount Washington, and like the previous victims, she had the telltale signs of having been bound at the ankles, wrists and neck. Lauren also had signs of being tortured, with burn marks on her hands.

Kimberly Martin

The next body was found on December 14 in a deserted lot near the City Hall. Kimberly Martin, a 17- year-old prostitute, had been working for a call girl agency as she feared being a victim of the Hillside Strangler. Tragically, the killers had happened to call the agency she was working for and book a girl, and Kimberly was the one sent out. Her naked body also showed signs of being tortured.

Cindy Hudspeth

The last known victim of the Hillside Stranglers was 20-year-old Cindy Hudspeth, who was a part-time waitress and student. Her orange Datsun vehicle had been located by a helicopter pilot where it had been abandoned over a cliff. When police arrived on the scene near Angeles Crest Highway, they located her body in the trunk of the car. Cindy had been tied up, tortured, raped and strangled before she was put in the trunk and the car pushed over the cliff.

Chasing the Killer

In January 1979, Bianchi had advertised a house-sitting job as a means to lure new victims. Two university students, Diane Wilder and Karen Mandic responded to the advertisement and agreed to meet with Bianchi, which proved to be a fatal mistake. Bianchi attacked both of the young women, raping them and strangling them before leaving them in Karen's car. But when the police searched the car after the bodies were discovered, they came across a piece of paper that had all the details of the arranged meeting with Bianchi written on it. Bianchi was brought in for questioning, and the officers realized very quickly that he was, in fact, the killer they were looking for.

Forensic evidence found in the car and at Bianchi's house tied him to the murders of the two students. Police identified the address in Los Angeles Bianchi had lived at previously, and when they contacted the LAPD, it was discovered that his MO for these murders matched that of the serial killer that had been known as the Hillside Strangler. On searching his home, police found a number of pieces of jewelry that had belonged to the Los Angeles victims, and forensic evidence from the home tied him to five of the unsolved Hillside murders. As a result, Bianchi was charged with first degree murder for each of those five victims in June 1979.

Bianchi tried everything he could think of to try and get off the murder charges. He attempted to convince the authorities that he suffered from multiple personality disorder, in the hopes of attaining an insanity defense. He even managed to convince several mental health experts, until one psychiatrist produced by the prosecution was able to trick Bianchi into creating more personalities, which exposed his lies.

As the police had been investigating Bianchi, they became aware of his cousin Buono, and noted that his upholstery business was close to where many of the bodies had been dumped. But they could not yet tie him to the murders, until Bianchi opened his mouth to save himself. Bianchi wanted to avoid the death penalty at any cost, and so he agreed to give testimony against Buono so he could be tried in LA, thereby avoiding the death penalty. He then produced a detailed statement implicating Buono in the LA murders and subsequently pleaded guilty to the five counts of murder. Police arrested Buono on October 22, and he was charged with ten counts of first degree murder.

Bianchi's trial was coming up soon, and he was still trying to find ways to get out of it. It also weighed heavily on his mind that he had effectively become an informer by turning in his cousin, and that this may have serious consequences to his wellbeing in prison. Those that nark are often targets of serious physical and sexual abuse, and sometimes they are even killed for informing on others. His next plan was to give contradictory statements regarding his pretrial testimony in the hopes that this would get the trial dismissed. The prosecution desperately needed Bianchi's testimony to prosecute Buono, and they almost gave in to Bianchi's plan, but the judge stepped in and insisted they proceed with the case as originally planned.

Trial by Jury

The trials were set to start in 1981, and they were going to take a long time to get through due to the number of victims and the amount of evidence the prosecution team had gathered. Fibers from Buono's upholstery business had been found on two of the victims, and another victim had rabbit hairs on her body that matched the rabbits Buono raised. Buono's wallet also had an imprint in the leather of the fake police badge they had used on numerous occasions to con prostitutes. Although Bianchi had agreed to testify against Buono as part of the plea deal, he was uncooperative throughout the trial.

Veronica Compton

While awaiting his trial, Bianchi had met and formed a relationship with a woman named Veronica Compton. She was a playwright and an actress who was obsessed with serial killers. Compton sent Bianchi a copy of a screenplay she had written, called The Mutilated Cutter, which was the story of a female serial killer. She had asked Bianchi what his thoughts were on the play, and thus a relationship developed between them as she became more and more fixated on him.

She would end up testifying on Bianchi's behalf for the defense during his trial. However, she was arrested after luring a woman to a motel and attempting to strangle her. The authorities believed it was a ruse to try and make them think the Hillside Strangler hadn't been caught after all, and that Bianchi therefore must be innocent. Bianchi was behind the whole idea, and he had managed to smuggle out some semen to Compton to place on the victim and make it look like a rape as well as a murder.

Compton was given a prison sentence, and she was eventually released in 2003.

Buono's trial lasted two years, from November 1981 until November 1983, which was the longest trial in legal history in America. At the end of the trial, Buono was found guilty of the ten murders he had been charged with. Bianchi had already pleaded guilty to five of the murders, and both men were sentenced to life in prison instead of the death penalty. Buono later ended up at Calipatria State Prison, and Bianchi was sent to the Washington State Penitentiary.

In 2002, Buono, who was much older than Bianchi, died of natural causes while in prison. Bianchi remains in prison to this day and cannot apply for parole until 2025.

Family Aftermath

Buono married once again in 1986, but this time it was from behind bars. His new wife was a supervisor from the California State Employment Development Department, named Christine

Kizuka. When Buono was found dead on September 21, 2002, it was believed he had suffered a heart attack, and he was alone in his cell at the time.

In 2007, Buono's former wife Mary Castillo was shot in the head and killed by their grandson, Christopher Buono. Shortly after committing the murder, Christopher committed suicide. He had grown up not knowing who his grandfather was, until he was finally told in 2005.

The Alphabet Killer – Was Bianchi the Elusive Killer?

There were two very different alphabet killer cases – one in New York and the other in California. The case that Bianchi appeared in during the investigation was the New York Alphabet Murders, which involved the savage killing of three young girls. Each of the girls had been raped and then strangled before being left out in the open for someone to find. The case was called the alphabet murders because of the initials of the girl's names.

Carmen Colon - found near Churchville

Carmen was just 10 years old when she went missing on November 16, 1971. Her body was found two days later in a gully, and she had been dead for about a day. Carmen had been sexually assaulted and then strangled. Her body and her neck were scarred by what appeared to be fingernail marks.

Michelle Maenza – found in Macedon

Eleven-year-old Michelle disappeared on November 26, 1973. Like Carmen, it would be two days before her body was found in Macedon, which was 15 miles from Rochester.

Wanda Walkowicz

Wanda was a cheery redhead who was sent out to buy some groceries for her mother on April 2, 1973. The 11-year-old made it to the store and purchased the food, and then vanished. Her body was found the following day near the base of an embankment in Webster. She had been raped and strangled, and it was possible the killer had used a belt to strangle her.

There were similar circumstances between these three murders and the ones in California, but they would later be determined to be the work of different killers. Investigators questioned hundreds of people, but nobody was ever caught. There was one man who was considered a person of interest, but he committed suicide. However, in 2007 he was ruled out through DNA profiling.

What makes this case so interesting and relevant to this chapter is that one suspect who has never been ruled out was Kenneth Bianchi. At the time of the murders, he was living in Rochester and working as an ice cream vendor. He would sell his wares from sites that were very close to the murder scenes of Carmen and Michelle. This all occurred before he moved to Los Angeles and became the Hillside Strangler with his cousin.

Although Bianchi has never been charged with these murders, circumstantial evidence exists that shows his car was seen at two of the crime scenes. Bianchi has tried repeatedly to get the investigators to clear him of these murders, but at this stage he is still a person of interest.

Two Minds Alike

It is not common to find two murderers working together, as it is usually a solo behavior. It is even less common for those two murderers to be members of the same family. Kenneth Bianchi and Angelo Buono were like-minded individuals that were brought together by family ties. When they collided in the same living environment, they shared their fantasies and set about satisfying their lust for sexual deviancy and murder.

It's unclear who the leader was and who was the follower. Although Buono was the older of the two, Bianchi was the charmer, the one who had the charisma and gift of the gab to gain the attention of women. Bianchi would later turn his own cousin Buono in to the authorities, and lay a lot of the blame at Buono's feet. But that was predominantly to save his own neck. He was offered a deal for his cooperation and he didn't hesitate to point the finger at Buono.

These two killers were sexual sadists who would place a plastic bag over their victim's head and bring them close to death over and over again before finally ending their misery via strangulation.

They had no regard for their victims in life or in death. They were dumped like trash on various hillsides, left naked for all to see. These women were shown no mercy and given no dignity when they were tossed asunder.

Both of these men would have continued to kill if Bianchi hadn't been caught. They had gotten away with it for a while and showed no signs of stopping at all. It's possible there are even more victims out there that haven't been discovered. With Buono's death, it is unlikely any more information will come forward, as Bianchi isn't going to divulge any further details for fear of being charged with more crimes. As it is, Bianchi has never been cleared of involvement with the Alphabet Killings. He vows he is innocent, but of course he would - more murder charges could lead to the death penalty.

Until they were identified as the killers, the Hillside Stranglers inflicted fear on the city. Women were being snatched off the streets and turning up dead in the hills, and nobody knew who the killers were or why they were committing the murders. Anybody could have been a victim. Yet despite this sense of fear, Bianchi and Buono were still able to find women to kidnap, torture and kill. Far too many people think it would never happen to them, that it happens to other people. But with killers like Bianchi and Buono, it indeed could have happened to anyone that crossed their paths.

Two killers, two family members, two sadists. They shared a home, they shared blood, and they shared a desire to kill. It's not clear if they ever killed separately before they moved in together. So, if they hadn't been related and moved in together, perhaps neither would have killed on their own.

Media

Films:

The Case of the Hillside Stranglers (1989)

The Hillside Strangler (2004)

Rampage: The Hillside Strangler Murders (2006)

CHAPTER 8:
Ronald Dominique
- The Bayou Strangler

For over a decade, the bodies of men had been turning up across four parishes in New Orleans, the victims of rape and murder. The number of victims would eventually reach 23 before a suspect was identified and found. As far as serial killers go, Ronald Dominique did not quite fit the bill physically and mentally. He wasn't a strong, active man – he was lazy and overweight. And he certainly did not have the charm of killers such as Bundy. But a serial killer he was, and he had devised a ruse to lure in his victims that enabled him to get away with it for such a long time. Ronald Dominique had a passion for raping men, but fearful of being caught, he decided to murder his victims thinking this would help him get away with it. Turns out, Dominique was very wrong.

Born In the Bayou

Dominique spent the majority of his childhood and youth living in Thibodaux, a small community on the bayou - the type of place where everybody knew everyone there in some way or another.

During his time at the local high school, Dominique was an active member of the glee club and could be found singing in the chorus. However, it was noticed early on that he was homosexual, and his classmates ridiculed him about it throughout his school years. Not once during that time did he admit to being gay.

As an adult, there were always two different sides to Dominique. On one hand he would help his neighbors with whatever they needed while he was living in various trailer parks. And on the other, he would frequent the local gay club dressed as a woman and do awful impersonations of Patti LaBelle. He couldn't seem to find where he belonged, though, and even the gay community who are hugely accepting of anyone did not find him particularly likable.

Dominique was constantly struggling with his finances, and would spend a lot of time living with his mother or other family members. In fact, just before he was arrested, Dominique had been living with his sister in a small trailer. He was suffering from problems with his heart, and he had to walk with a cane for support.

Because he liked to help people, Dominique had joined the local Lions Club a few months before he was arrested. He would go on Sunday afternoons and help the senior citizens by calling out the Bingo numbers. He was actually well liked by those at the Lions Club, and it seemed he had finally found somewhere he could be accepted. At the time of his arrest, Dominique had moved out of his sister's trailer and into a homeless shelter. Although it's not certain why he did this, it is suggested that it was because of the effect the police surveillance of him was having on his family.

Criminal Record

Dominique had come into contact with the police on numerous occasions for a variety of criminal charges. These included:

June 12 1985

Charged with telephone harassment.

May 15 1994

Charged with speeding and driving while intoxicated.

August 25 1996

Arrested on charges of forcible rape and given a bond of $100,000. A partially naked young man had escaped from Dominique's home and screamed that he had tried to murder him. Unfortunately, when the case was brought before the court, the victim could not be located. The case was continued indefinitely in November.

May 19 2000

Charged with disturbing the peace and given a fine.

February 10 2002

Arrested and charged with assault against a woman during the Mardi Gras parade. An argument broke out between them over Dominique accusing the woman of hitting a baby stroller while in the parking lot. She apologized, but Dominique verbally abused her, then slapped her face. Instead of going to trial, he enrolled in an offender's program, which he completed in October of the same year.

Murder to Avoid Prison!

Because of his previous experiences with law enforcement, Dominique tried to come up with a plan that would ensure he could continue to rape men without the threat of getting caught. He decided the only way would be to kill his victims, thereby removing any potential witnesses. Dominique clearly didn't think this through completely because, by dumping the bodies in easily accessible places, he was leaving the police plenty of clues that would ultimately lead to his downfall.

Almost all of Dominique's 23 victims had led difficult lives, many of them plagued with drug addictions and previous clashes with law enforcement. Some of the men he killed had been homeless, so their disappearances often weren't reported until sometime later, if at all. His victims ranged in age from 17 to 46, but the majority were in their 20s. He also seemed to either have a preference for black men or perhaps they were easier targets, because 18 of his victims were black.

The cause of death couldn't always be established, but for those where it could be, their deaths were due to asphyxiation or strangulation. Some of the victims had been beaten, and they were sometimes found naked. When Dominique approached a potential victim, he had two methods of luring them, depending on their sexuality. If the man was homosexual, Dominique would simply request them to agree to be tied up as part of the deal for sexual favors. If the man was heterosexual, Dominique would produce a photograph of a woman he claimed to be his wife who was shy but liked her sexual partners to be tied up. Either way, the deal was always that the man would have to agree to let Dominique tie them. If they refused, he moved on and looked for another suitable victim.

The first two victims were David Levron Mitchell, 19, and Gary Pierre, 20, and they were killed in 1997. Police found David's body near Hahnville, and Gary's body in St. Charles Parish. The next year, another three victims were found. First, Larry Ranson, 38, was found in July, and then Oliver LeBanks, 17, was discovered in October. Dominique continued to rape and murder men for the next nine years, until his final known victim, Chris Sutterfield, 27, was killed in 2006. The number of victims was now at 23.

David Levron Mitchell – (19) – 1997

Gary Pierre – (20) – 1997

Larry Ranson – (38) – 1998

Oliver 'Boe' LeBanks – (27) – 1998

Manuel Reed – (19) – 1999

Mitchell Johnson – 1999

Kurt Michael Cunningham – (23)

Anoka Jones – (26) – 2002

Wayne Smith – (17) – 2005

Datrell Woods – (18) – 2003

Michael Barnett – (20)

Leon Paul 'T-Paul' Lirette – (22) – 2005

August Watkins – (31)

Nicholas 'T-Nick' Pellegrin – (21)

Chris Deville

Kenneth Randolph

Alonzo Hogan

Christopher Charles Sutterfield – (27) 2006

Some of the dates of death and ages of the victims are unconfirmed.

Caught and Prosecuted

With such a large number of victims being found, a multi-jurisdictional task force was created in 2005 to work on the cases and ultimately catch what was now being referred to as the Bayou Serial Killer or the Bayou Strangler. The task force was led by State Attorney General Charles Foti and was made up of law enforcement officers from right across the bayou country in Louisiana.

In 2006, the task force received information regarding the murders from a probation and parole agent after one of his parolees had mentioned an encounter he had with a man 4 or 5 years earlier. The parolee claimed he had been approached by a man who was living in a camper and had been offered to have sex with the man's wife provided he would agree to be tied up. He followed him back to the camper on Bayou Blue Road, but he felt nervous and fled.

This information led police to Ronald Dominique as being the man in the camper. As they investigated further, they discovered he had been arrested back in 1996 on a charge of raping a man. He was held in jail for three months before the case was due to go to court, but it was subsequently dismissed because the victim had disappeared and, therefore could not testify.

The police were able to track Dominique down to a homeless shelter, and when asked to provide a DNA sample, he complied. His DNA was subsequently matched to two murders in the Jefferson Parish. On December 1, 2006, Dominique was formally charged with first degree murder. But it wouldn't be long before many more charges were added. He would eventually be charged with eight more counts of aggravated rape and murder.

Dominique was questioned for two days about the murders, during which time he made the shocking confession that he had actually raped and killed 23 men. He claimed he never physically fought his victims; he instead waited until they were tied up and helpless. There were never any drugs used to subdue his victims either. His choice of victim also meant there was a lesser chance of them being reported missing quickly, so he could easily dispose of the body without having to rush. He dumped the bodies over the wide area of six parishes to prevent the cases from being linked straight away.

During his interviews with the police, Dominique claimed to be suffering from serious heart disease and mobility issues, and he had to rely on a cane to walk. Many of the officers believed this to be yet another ploy to try and gain sympathy, in the hopes that he could persuade a jury he was physically unable to kill and dispose of the murder victims. But the DNA match could not be disputed, and despite his alleged health problems, Dominique was most definitely the guilty party.

The lead prosecutor assigned to the case was Assistant District Attorney Mark Rhodes. It was to be a challenging experience because, although he was only being charged at first for eight of the murders, they still needed to provide evidence for the other 15. This involved a massive amount of information to collect and analyze. The defense attorney was Richard Goorley, who worked with the Capital Assistance Project. Whenever there is a capital murder case, the project has a contract with the Public Defender Board to handle them.

As the trial date fast approached, the defense was forced to request a motion to stay the proceedings due to Dominique's health. It turned out he did have a problem with his heart and now needed bypass surgery. To proceed with the motion, Dominique had to undergo a medical examination by an independent specialist and sign his health records over to the state. He was then granted the time required for the surgery to be performed.

When it finally came time for Dominique to appear in court, he was 44 years of age and wore shackles on his feet and around his waist. He had pleaded guilty to all charges, and as the judge read out the names, charges and imposed sentences for each of the eight victims, Dominique stood with his head bowed down. He was sentenced to eight consecutive life terms.

Dominique was incarcerated at the Louisiana State Penitentiary in Angola, and placed in a single cell where he spends 23 hours out of each day. For one hour a day, he can either go for a shower or have some recreation time. Because of the nature of his crimes and the media attention his crimes attracted, Dominique is housed in the cell block until it is safe for him to be put in with the general population in the prison. However, that is not likely to happen anytime soon, if ever.

Since he was incarcerated, there have been two write-ups placed on his record for behavior issues. One of the incidents involved him throwing hot water at an inmate, which fortunately didn't hit him. The second incident, Dominique was caught throwing soap bars into another man's cell. The prison has acknowledged that Dominique is not good at getting along with other people, and people struggle to get along with him.

The Two Faces of Ronald

When news broke in Dominique's home town that he was the one responsible for so many horrible murders, people were completely shocked. To most he seemed to be a good man, always willing to help his friends and neighbors, and a doting uncle. The other side of Dominique was a deviant and sadistic killer who saw his victims as nothing more than a means for him to satisfy his desires and urges.

Ronnie Hebert, who owned a bar called Ronnie's Lounge, had known Dominique for many years. At one point in time, he had dated a cousin of Dominique's and came into contact with him on several occasions. A few years back, Dominique would hang out at Hebert's bar nearly every weekend, but he generally kept to himself. He very rarely drank alcohol and would normally just play pool and drink sodas. He certainly never caused any problems while he was in the bar.

A woman who owned the local video rental store near where Dominique parked his trailer was very familiar with him as he was a regular customer of hers. She had always thought of him as being a very friendly man, and she was aware he was gay because he often rented homosexual pornographic movies and would talk to her about some of the dates he went on with men. Shortly before he was arrested, he walked into the store one day and told her he was a suspect in the serial killer murders. She didn't believe it for a second and joked with him about it. Once he was arrested, that conversation left a haunting memory in her mind.

Nobody who knew Dominique had ever seen him on a date or with a partner. He is not an attractive man, being overweight and unhealthy. They couldn't even really recall him having any friends. This made the conversation with the owner of the video store even more ominous – perhaps when he was talking with her about his dates, he was really talking about his murders.

The Effect on the Gay Community

Dominique's confessions to the murders shocked everyone, including those who knew him in the gay community. They have been left with deep concerns that the public may react badly to all homosexuals in the district now that they know Dominique is gay. The community is also spooked that they had a serial killer amongst them and they didn't know.

Although Dominique socialized in the gay community, he was not a popular man. Many people just didn't like him. Dominique was often referred to by the community as 'Miss Moped' after he won a moped through a McDonald's competition and would ride it around as transportation. Just like when he was a child, Dominique was still the target of teasing as a grown man.

Despite so many young gay men disappearing, the gay community was never greatly concerned about being potential victims. They realized that the killer was targeting homeless and troubled men on the streets rather than those who sat in the local bar and played pool.

Homosexual Serial Killers

Although homosexual serial killers may not seem that common, there have certainly been some throughout history, dating right back to Alexander the Great. When it comes to murder, sexuality doesn't determine how violent you may be or why you kill. It only really plays a part in choosing victims. Listed below are some of the more sadistic and prolific homosexual serial killers in modern history. Of course Fritz Haarmann and Hans Grans also belong on this list, but their story is in a previous chapter.

Luis Alfredo Garavito

Nicknamed 'the beast', Garavito is perhaps one of the worst serial killers known, regardless of sexuality. Garavito was born in Colombia in 1957, and he raped, tortured, killed and mutilated 140 young boys over a seven-year period, from 1992 to 1999. He would lure the children to him under the pretense of giving them food. His method of killing was by screwdriver or knife, or sometimes both at the same time. Garavito confessed to his crimes and admitted there were many more. He subsequently provided the authorities with a map showing the locations of over 300 bodies. He is serving a 1,853-year sentence in prison.

John Wayne Gacy

One of the most well-known serial killers and despite being married at one point, John Wayne Gacy was a prolific predator of young men and teenage boys. Gacy sexually assaulted his victims, then murdered them inside his home. Most of his victims were lured to his house by either deception or force, and apart from the first victim who was stabbed to death, the majority were strangulated or asphyxiated. Twenty-six of his victims ended up buried beneath his home in the crawl space, with three others buried on the property and four thrown in the river.

Gacy was known as the Killer Clown because he used to dress up as a clown and entertain sick children at the local hospital. This was in stark contrast to his life as a fairly successful businessman and a sadistic serial killer. Gacy was convicted of committing 33 murders and received the death sentence for 12 of them. He sat on death row for 14 years and was executed on May 10, 1994.

Patrick Wayne Kearney

Born in 1939, Kearney became known as the Freeway Killer, and he would prey on young men during the 1970s in California. When caught, Kearney claimed to have killed up to forty-three victims, but he was only ever charged with twenty-one, as police were unable to corroborate the evidence needed to prosecute for the others.

Huang Yong

Yong was born in China in 1974, in the Henan Province. He would stalk his victims in video arcades and internet cafes, and it is believed he is responsible for killing up to 25 young men. He would keep their belts as souvenirs and buried their bodies on his property. He was charged with 17 murders and was sentenced to death. His execution took place in November 2003.

Jeffrey Lionel Dahmer

Yet another well-known killer, Jeffrey Dahmer began his raping and killing spree when he was just 18 years old. Dahmer preferred teenage boys as they were easier to control and dominate, and he would frequent local gay bars looking for the ideal victims. He would kidnap his victims, then drug them, then rape, kill and eat them. He also had a penchant for having sex with the dead bodies. Dahmer is possibly the most disturbed killer, and he was convicted of 15 murders and sent to prison. He was himself murdered by an inmate.

David Edward Maust

Born in 1954, Maust professed himself to be a homosexual murderer of young boys. He had received psychiatric care as a child and was considered to be deeply troubled. He was charged with the murders of five boys, and in January 2006, he committed suicide.

Randy Steven Kraft

Kraft was born in California in 1945, and was an intelligent man who ended up getting high security clearances from the Air Force. But outside of work, Kraft enjoyed posing on his couch with his gay lover and his victims, and took numerous photos. These would end up becoming evidence when he was arrested and convicted of committing 16 murders between the years of 1972 and 1983. Authorities believe he may be responsible for another 51 murders of young men. Convicted in 1989, Kraft is still sitting on death row awaiting his execution date.

A Dangerous Mind

Ronald Dominique was not your average homosexual. He had a perverse need to tie his victims up so he could rape them as he pleased before killing them. But he hadn't always been a killer. He had been caught before for raping a young man but had never been formally charged. This alone should have put him on the radar of the police, yet he was able to later kill a number of men before his name was even thought of.

After his previous experience with the law, Dominique wanted to continue raping young men, but he didn't want to go to prison for it. So he came up with the plan that if he killed them, they couldn't tell tales and he wouldn't be caught. This may have seemed like a good idea to him at the time, but he never considered that he could be linked to the victims forensically once their bodies were found.

Dominique was a joke among the gay community. He was fat, balding, and unattractive, and he managed to make a fool of himself at the local bar where the members of the gay community would socialize. He seemed incapable of normal human relationships, and perhaps this is why he felt the need to trick his victims into coming back to his place. By tying them up, not only could they not run away, they would also have to endure whatever pain and suffering he chose to inflict on them. To Dominique, it was easier that way than to go out on a proper date and risk being rejected.

167

Dominique lived from welfare check to welfare check, often having to live with his sister because he claimed to be physically disabled. Whatever ailment he had, it certainly didn't stop him from physically restraining his victims, then getting rid of their bodies. What money he had he spent at the bar or at the local video store, hiring hordes of gay pornographic movies. Everyone in the community knew he was gay and thought he was a bit strange, but nobody had a clue what he was really doing.

Like many other serial killers, Dominique was careful about the victims he selected. He predominantly chose men who were homeless, drug addicts, or those willing to sell their bodies for a price. He chose men that could go missing for days, even months, without being noticed. Would he kill again if the opportunity presented itself? Absolutely, though he would likely come up with yet another plan to try and prevent capture. Thankfully, Dominique will never see the sunshine outside of the prison walls ever again.

Media

Film:

Bayou Blue (2011)

Book:

Ronald Dominique – Serial Killers Unauthorized and Uncensored – T.J. Carlson

More books by Jack Rosewood

SAVE $32 by getting this boxed set of eight (8) books instead of buying them one by one!

- Cousins David Alan Gore and Fred Waterfield, who found at an early age that both shared sick sexual fantasies of rape and murder and sought out victims to fulfill those fantasies;

- Australian serial killer Eric Edgar Cooke, who selected his victims and his methods of murder at random, shooting some, stabbing others, until he was finally hanged, the last man to face the gallows in Perth;

- William Heirens, who went from being the most popular boy in his class to a murderer who was completely out of a control, even going so far as to leave a desperate message at one scene, written in lipstick: "For heavens sake catch me before I kill more. I cannot control myself";

- Belle Gunness, a stocky Norwegian woman who cold-bloodedly killed several of her children, husbands and suitors in order to obtain their life insurance policies and cash – or eliminate witnesses, burying most in wooden trunks beneath the hog pen;

- Joseph Paul Franklin, who confessed to the attempted murder of Hustler magazine publisher Larry Flynt and killed multiple others – most often interracial couples - as his own personal form of "racial cleansing," inspired by reading Hitler's "Mein Kampf";

- John Christie, a slender but sadistic killer whose British flat was found stuffed with dead bodies including that of his own wife, who was discovered buried beneath the floorboards, when he was finally arrested in 1950s;

- Patrick Wayne Kearney, who killed young men hitching through California in the 1970s, usually with a bullet to the back of the head, then had sex with their dead bodies; and

- Jerry Brudos, who sadistically murdered several young women after torturing them in his family's garage, saving ghoulish mementos including a foot he kept in the freezer, which he brought out like a toy in order to display it in stolen high heels, masturbating from the sheer pleasure of it all.

The world can be a very strange place in general and when you open the pages of this true crime anthology you will quickly learn that the criminal world specifically can be as bizarre as it is dangerous. In the following book, you will be captivated by mysterious missing person cases that defy all logic and a couple cases of murderous mistaken identity. Follow along as detectives conduct criminal investigations in order to solve cases that were once believed to be unsolvable. Every one of the crime cases chronicled in the pages of this book are as strange and disturbing as the next.

The twelve true crime stories in this book will keep you riveted as you turn the pages, but they will probably also leave you with more questions than answers. For instance, you will be left pondering how two brothers from the same family could disappear with no trace in similar circumstances over ten years apart. You will also wonder how two women with the same first and last names, but with no personal connections, could be murdered within the same week in the same city. The examination of a number of true crime murder cases that went cold, but were later solved through scientific advances, will also keep you intrigued and reading.

Open the pages of this book, if you dare, to read some of the most bizarre cases of disappearances, mistaken identity, and true murder. Some of the cases will disturb and anger you, but make no mistake, you will want to keep reading!

GET THESE BOOKS FOR FREE

Go to www.jackrosewood.com

and get these E-Books for free!

A Note From The Author

Hello, this is Jack Rosewood. Thank you for reading this book. I hope you enjoyed the read. If you did, I'd appreciate if you would take a few moments to post a review on Amazon.

I would also love if you'd sign up to my newsletter to receive updates on new releases, promotions and a FREE copy of my Herbert Mullin E-Book, visit www.JackRosewood.com

Thanks again for reading this book, make sure to follow me on Facebook.

Best Regards

Jack Rosewood

CPSIA information can be obtained
at www.ICGtesting.com
Printed in the USA
BVHW042138070521
606845BV00014B/397

9 781542 957786